Guide To The Recommended

COUNTRY INNS
Of New England

Guests—

Ye are welcome here,
    be at your ease
Go to bed when you're ready
    get up when you please.
Happy to share with you
    such as we've got
The leak in the roof
    the soup in the pot.
Ye don't have to thank us,
    or laugh at our jokes
Sit deep and come often
    you're one of the folks.

found in an inn, Brookline Mass

EIGHTH EDITION

Guide To The Recommended

COUNTRY INNS

Of New England

Elizabeth Squier

Illustrated by Olive Metcalf

To
Gary + Elaine
May 21, 1983
Bill + Julie

The Globe Pequot Press

Chester, Connecticut 06412

Library of Congress Number: 73–83255
ISBN:0-87106-976-8
Manufactured in the United States of America
Eighth Edition

First Edition, 1974
Second Edition, 1976
Third Edition, 1977
Fourth Edition, 1978
Fifth Edition, 1979
Sixth Edition, 1980
Seventh Edition, 1981

Book design by Barbara Marks

Contents

Dedicated to
Robert W. Wilkerson,
with love

How this guide is arranged

The inns are listed by states, and alphabetically by towns within each state. The states are arranged by a peculiar whim of the publisher in the following order: Connecticut, Rhode Island, Massachusetts, Vermont, New Hampshire, and Maine. Before each state listing is a map and special index to help you in planning a trip, and on page 373 is a complete index of every inn in the book.

The abbreviations - The following abbreviations are used:

    EP - European Plan—Room without meals.

    EPB - European Plan—Room with full breakfast.

    AP - American Plan—Room with all meals.

    MAP - Modified American Plan—
        Room with breakfast and dinner.

    BYOB - Bring Your Own Bottle.

The pointing fingers - In the write-ups you will, from time to time, find some pointing fingers ☞ ☞ ☞ ☞ ☞. While I have not rated the inns, when I found something particularly outstanding or different, I inserted a ☞ as a special note.

And the E symbol - At the end of some of the write-ups you will find this symbol:

    E - Stands for Elizabeth

This was to give me the opportunity to add an individual note on a special, personal delight.

How to enjoy this guide

When I first started writing *The Guide To The Recommended Country Inns Of New England* back in 1973, I had no idea that there were so many people who were tired of the monotony of motels and thruway hotels, who were willing to exchange certain conveniences for the infinitely more warming pleasure of a good country inn.

Although I make every attempt to keep this guide up-to-date, please realize that prices and menus are subject to change, as are innkeepers. If you are planning to stay overnight, or even to have a special dinner out, I recommend that you call ahead for reservations so that you will not be disappointed. Many of the inns are quite small, and it would be a shame to travel a long distance and not get in.

By my descriptions and comments I have tried to indicate whether an inn would be appropriate for children, pets, young couples, or elderly folk. But do not forget that the very reason you are passing up a motel or a hotel is for the bit of adventure and surprise you will find sitting in a weathered farmhouse, eating country cooking, chatting with a discovered friend, and finding new delight in a very old tradition.

With prices fluctuating so widely in today's economy I now quote you an inn's current low and high rates only. This will give you a good indication, though not exact, of the prices you can expect. Also, the inns in the ski country and many along the shoreline have package rates. When you call, do inquire about them.

About pets: Most of the inns do not accept pets, but give an inn a call before you go. Many times they can make arrangements for you.

And do not become distressed because an inn you like may not be in this book. Please understand that my definition of a country inn is that it *must* have lodging, as well as good food, and *must* be open essentially year round. It is all right, however, if it closes for a month or a bit more for refurbishing, or, as an instance, to avoid the uniquely New England "mud season" of late winter. With the skyrocketing cost of oil several more northerly inns have had to extend their closing periods. I have eased the rules a bit to keep these good inns in the book. If you have an inn recommendation, please write me so that I can review it for the next edition.

And a special note hopefully to dispel a rumor that has been going about. There is no charge of any kind for an inn to be in this guide.

So, enjoy! This GUIDE was compiled for you, fellow lovers of New England Country Inns.

Elizabeth

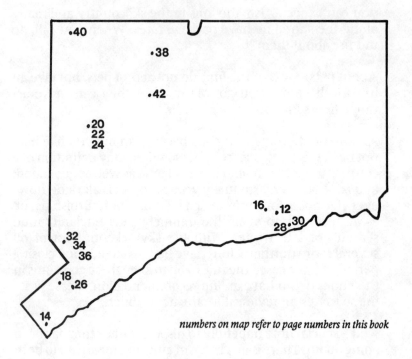

numbers on map refer to page numbers in this book

Connecticut

Griswold Inn
Essex, Connecticut
06426

Innkeepers: Bill and Victoria Winterer
Telephone: 203-767-0991
Rooms: 19, all with private bath; three suites.
Rates: $42, double occupancy; $48 to $50, suites; continental
breakfast included.
Facilities: Open all year. Closed Christmas Eve and Christmas
Day. Lunch, dinner, children's menu, bar. All major
credit cards accepted.

Essex is a special place, and "The Gris" is one of the
things that makes this river town so appealing. Essex, though
settled long before the Revolution, is still a living, breathing,
working place, not a recreated museum of a town. The first
warship of the Continental Navy, the *Oliver Cromwell*, was
built and commissioned here in 1776.

When you come in from the cold to the welcome
of ☛ crackling fireplaces, you are doing what others have
done before you for 200 years. You can lunch or dine in the
cool dimness of the Library, or the Gun Room. A special spot

is the Steamboat Room where the ☞ mural on the far wall floats gently, making you feel that you are really on the river. Their collection of ☞ Currier & Ives is museum-size and quality. ☞ There is music almost every night, old time banjoes, sea chanteys, Dixieland jazz, or just good piano; but ☞ never rock 'n roll.

The rooms are old, but nice. The *Oliver Cromwell* suite is in the main building, with a wood-burning fireplace, comfortable couches, a four-poster bed, and a lovely bar for your very own. There is a very nice view of Middle Cove from here.

In the bar is a great, old-fashioned popcorn machine. Bill Winterer gives popcorn to all ☞ the children who come in. Do ask for some. It's one of many personal touches that make this nice kind of inn such a special place.

Upriver in Middletown Bill has another inn, the Town Farms Inn. At this time there are no rooms, but the food is divine.

And down the river in Old Saybrook Bill owns the Dock and Dine, a fine seafood restaurant.

How to get there: Take the Connecticut Turnpike to Exit 69, and follow Route 9 north to Exit 3. Turn left at the bottom of ramp to a traffic light, turn right and follow this street right through town to the river. The inn is on your right, about 100 yards before you get to the river.

E: *My favorite thing about The Gris? Love that popcorn machine in the bar.*

The Homestead Inn
Greenwich, Connecticut
06830

Innkeepers: Lessie Davison and Nancy Smith
Telephone: 203-869-7500
Rooms: 13, all with private bath and TV; two suites.
Rates: $65, single; $85 to $105, double; $105 to $132, suite;
 continental breakfast included.
Facilities: Inn open all year. Dining room closed Good Friday,
 Christmas, New Year's Day, and Labor Day. Lunch Mon-
 day through Friday, dinner seven days a week, bar. All
 major credit cards accepted.

Jacques Thiebeult, the French chef who oversees the
superb food in the inn restaurant, called La Grange, should
receive many stars.

Let us start with the hors d'oeuvres, eight of them, from
mushrooms marinated in a Madagascar pepper sauce, little
necks baked with duxelles and herbs, to pâté. Soups are
scrumptious. The Billi-Bi is a hot mussel soup. If you are
lucky they will have the ☛Crème de Laiture, a velvet
blend of lettuce and peas. The entrees are beef, veal,

☞ poached mousse of salmon napped with a creamy champagne sauce, plus daily specials. As for the desserts, the ☞ White Chocolate Mousse is the best I have ever eaten, and the Gâteau Belle Haven will make you think you are in heaven. Need I say more.

The inn's rooms are beautifully refurbished and each has a name. The Poppy Room is a single with the smallest bathtub I believe was ever made. The Tassle Room has his and her desks, the Sleigh Room has old sleigh beds, and the Robin Room has ☞ delicate stencils on the wall. They were found under six layers of wallpaper dating back to 1860. The Bride's Room has a queen-sized, canopy bed. All have electric blankets, televisions, and clock radios.

And for a quiet drink to end a day there is no finer spot than the bar. It is called, rather nicely, The Chocolate Bar.

How to get there: Going north or south on I-95, take Exit 3. Go north about 200 yards to a light, turn left on Horseneck Road, go to the dead end, and turn left. Go under the turnpike and up a hill. The inn is on your right.

E: *The ironstone place settings in Wedgewood's Chinese Bird pattern and the beautiful stemware are for me.*

> *A well run inn and a man on a diet*
> *go together about as well as*
> *an arsonist and a bale of hay.*

Copper Beech Inn
Ivoryton, Town of Essex, Connecticut
06442

Innkeepers: Paul and Louise Ebeltoft
Telephone: 203-767-0330
Rooms: Five, all with private bath.
Rates: $55 to $85, double occupancy, continental breakfast
   included.
Facilities: Open all year. Closed Mondays, Christmas Eve,
   Christmas Day, and New Year's Day. Lunch, dinner.
   Greenhouse cocktail lounge open Tuesday through
   Sunday in season, and Friday through Sunday out of
   season. All major credit cards accepted.

The magnificent copper beech tree that shades the front
lawn of this wonderful inn was inspiration for the name.

The rooms are charming, with antiques, comfortable
beds, and unbelievable old-fashioned bathrooms. Lots
of 🐄 soft towels are a real plus.

The four dining rooms have comfortable Chippendale
or Queen Anne chairs. The dining porch, which is my favorite, is done in white wicker. The 🐄 spacious tables are

16

spread far apart for gracious dining. Fresh flowers are everywhere, and the waiters serving the excellent Four Star fare are friendly and efficient.

There are at least 15 or 16 appetizers to start the menu, each one better than the next. The soups that follow are superb. The lobster bisque has chunks of lobster in it, as it should. The chilled Billi-Bi is excellent. Lunch at the inn is fun and very good. Dinner by candlelight is perfection. The menu changes three or four times a year, but to give you an idea: salmon in puff pastry with sole mousse and a salmon sauce suprême, or medallions of veal, or one of my very favorites, Chateaubriand, tender tenderloin of beef surrounded by fresh vegetables.

And for dessert there are about 16 choices, all made fresh here at the inn. Do try the white chocolate mousse. I like it here, as I think you can tell.

How to get there: The inn has recently added limousine service from open marinas, bus, trains, and local airports. If you're driving, the inn is located one mile west of Connecticut Route 9, from Exit 3 or 4. Follow the signs to Ivoryton. The inn is on Ivoryton's Main Street, on the left side.

E: *A turkey sandwich to go after a sumptuous dinner is my idea of a perfect Thanksgiving.*

One good night in a country inn can keep the mind in quiet order for many moons.

The Roger Sherman Inn
New Canaan, Connecticut
06840

Innkeepers: Katherine Maliszewski and Steve Zur
Telephone: 203-966-4541
Rooms: 12, all with private bath, air conditioning, and TV; six
    apartments available by the month.
Rates: $40, single; $50 to $65, double; EP.
Facilities: Open all year. Closed Sundays. Breakfast for house
    guests only. Lunch, dinner, bar. Parking. Nature center
    and theater nearby. All major credit cards accepted.

Built in 1740, and once the home of Roger Sherman,
one of the signers of the Declaration of Independence, this
friendly inn still offers a warm welcome to the tired traveler.
The cuisine may be a bit more continental than it was in the
early days, but we are all a bit more sophisticated today.
There is music in the dining room here on the weekend.
    If you are so inclined, there is a wonderful nature center
just across the street from the inn, and the summer theater at
Westport is a popular place to go on a warm evening.
    The guest rooms are large and comfortable. There are

even two and three-room apartments, so you can bring the whole family and stay a month. In the summer there is "Veranda Dining." In winter, lead me to the Publick Tap Room.

New Canaan is a lovely little town with some very attractive shops, among them one of the very best bakeries I have ever run across. There is a good book shop, some fine dress shops, and antique shops. There is also a place called "Fat Tuesday," rumored to be the mecca for all local swingers.

If you want a nice place to hole up for a week or a month, give The Roger Sherman a try. The food is good, and the surroundings delightful.

How to get there: Take exit 37 from the Merritt Parkway and follow Route 124 north through New Canaan. One-half mile beyond the town you will find the inn on your right.

One good night in a country inn
can keep the mind in quiet order
for many moons.

olive Metcalf

Boulders Inn
New Preston, Connecticut
06777

Innkeepers: Carolyn and Jameson Woollen
Telephone: 203-868-7918
Rooms: 15, all with private bath; eight with fireplace.
Rates: $51 to $63, single; $78 to $98, double; MAP.
Facilities: Open all year. Breakfast, lunch in summer only.
Dinner daily in summer, Tuesday through Saturday
from November to Memorial Day. Sunday brunch
served from Labor Day to Memorial Day. Bar. Swim-
ming, boating, tennis, bicycling, hiking, and cross-
country skiing nearby. MasterCard and Visa accepted.

The stone boulders from which the inn was made jut
right into the inn, and so the name, Boulders Inn.
Pinnacle Mountain behind the inn offers hiking trails,
and Clea, the inn dog, will guide you up the mountain, but
beware, for she is apt to leave you to find your own way
down. From the top of Pinnacle the climber is rewarded with
a ☛ panorama that includes New York state to the west and
Massachusetts to the north.

The guest rooms all have a view either of the lake or the woods and are tastefully furnished. ☞ Eight of the rooms have fireplaces. The living room is spacious, has large windows and comfortable chairs and couches, and is a nice place for tea or cocktails. There is an outside terrace where, in summer, you may enjoy cocktails, dinner, and ☞ marvelous sunsets.

The food is excellent with all baking done right here. The desserts are grand. Brunch has one entree that sounds especially yummy, Chicken Cashew Crepe. Dinner has several entrees. One favorite is Boeuf Bourguignon, morsels of beef sauteed in cognac and baked in a rich sauce of burgundy wine, fresh mushrooms, and herbs.

How to get there: From New York take I-84 to Route 7 in Danbury and follow it north to New Milford. Take a right onto Route 202 to New Preston. Take a left onto Route 45 and you will find the inn as you round onto the lake.

E: *Tweek is a black inn cat. Curl up in a chair with a book and Tweek will join you.*

In the autumn, especially as one ages,
a firelit tavern in an excellent inn cannot be bettered
by the smallest mansions in Christendom.

The Hopkins Inn
on Lake Waramaug
New Preston, Connecticut
06777

Innkeepers: Franz and Beth Schober
Telephone: 203-868-7295
Rooms: Nine, seven with private bath; one apartment.
Rates: $31 to $42, double occupancy, EP.
Facilities: Inn open May to November. Restaurant closed
   January through March. Breakfast for house guests
   only, lunch, dinner, bar, lounge. Private beach on lake.
   Golf, tennis, and horseback riding nearby. No credit
   cards accepted.

Overlooking lovely Lake Waramaug sits this inn surrounded by majestic trees on particularly beautiful grounds.
The inn has glorious, unmatched views of the lake.
   In season there is ☛ dining under the magnificent
maple and horse chestnut trees, and dine you will. The inn
has a ☛ trout pond where you can pick the fish you fancy,
and next you have Trout Meunière; fresher fish would be

hard to find.

Franz is the chef, and a few of his specials include Lamb Curry, Veal Piccata or Milanaise, and Boeuf Bourguignon. Those are for lunch. For dinner how about bay scallops in a special garlic sauce, and backhendl with lingonberries. And there is always a special or two.

The dining rooms are cheerful. The fireplace has ceramic square tiles across the mantle, and the decorations are wine racks full of wines from all over the world. Naturally their wine list is quite impressive and, pleasantly, fairly priced.

There is a private beach down at the lake for use by inn guests. Bicycling, hiking, horseback riding, golf, and tennis are available nearby.

The rooms are very clean, neat and country-inn comfortable. Almost all of the rooms have a view of the lake.

How to get there: Take I-84 to Route 202 east to Route 45 in New Preston. Turn left on Route 45 and follow it 2 miles past the lake. Take your first left after the lake. Then take the second right onto Hopkins Road.

E: Strawberries Romanoff, Meringue Glacé, Coupe aux Marrons, and homemade cheesecake. Need I say more.

*"The best landscape in the world
is improved by a good inn in the foreground."*
— Dr. Samuel Johnson

The Inn on Lake Waramaug
New Preston, Connecticut
06777

Innkeepers: Dick and Bobbie Combs
Telephone: 203-868-0563, 212-724-8775
Rooms: 25, all have private bath, air conditioning, and TV.
Rates: $61 to $78, per person, double occupancy, MAP. Package plans available.
Facilities: Open all year. Closed on Christmas. Breakfast, lunch, dinner, bar. Indoor pool, sauna, game room, cross-country skiing, ice-skating, boating, lake swimming. Tennis, golf, horseback riding, and downhill skiing nearby. All major credit cards accepted.

The second largest natural lake in Connecticut fills part of the view you have from this old Colonial inn that dates back to 1795. There are enormous 100-year-old sugar maples and a magnificent Hawthorn tree that was in full bloom when I was last there.

There is so much to do here both inside and outside the inn. Winter is a fairyland. The innkeepers keep an 🐾 area on the lake cleared for skating. Cross-country skiing starts just outside the door. Downhill skiing is but 20 minutes away. And how about a horse-drawn sleigh ride, compliments of the inn. Summer brings boating and swimming, or just enjoying the shaded lawns and sandy beach. The inn has a showboat that takes you around the lake. A nice way to see it all. Bicycles are also available. Nearby are golf, tennis, and horseback riding.

Inside the inn is year-round fun. A heated swimming pool with a whirlpool lagoon plus a sauna snuggle up to the Barefoot Bar. The game room has pool, Ping-Pong, electronic and other games, and even a juke box.

The Sand Bar on the patio at the beach is open in summer. During winter's blustery weather a glowing fireplace in the inn and drinks from Dudley's Tavern will keep you warm.

The dining rooms are large and well appointed, serving good food all year round. On one occasion I had Steak Diane, tender beef laced with brandy, mustard, and mushrooms, and oh, so good.

For antique lovers there is a gracious old fireplace made from the bricks that once were ballast on English sailing ships.

This is a wonderful place for the whole family or just one tired "inn creeper" like me. I arrived at a long day's end and spent about an hour in the pool. What a way to relax.

How to get there: From New York take I-84 to Route 7 in Danbury and follow it north to New Milford. Take a right onto Route 202 to New Preston. Take Route 45 west and follow signs to the inn. From Boston take the Massachusetts Turnpike to I-86. Follow it to I-84. Exit from I-84 onto Route 4 in Farmington. Continue on Route 4 to Route 118, and in Litchfield, pick up Route 202 and follow it to Route 45 west.

E: *Zeke and Panda, the inn animals, are wonderful. Edgar is the cat. There are also three ponies, Chester, Happy, and Merry Legs.*

—Olive Metcalf

Silvermine Tavern
Norwalk, Connecticut
06850

Innkeeper: Francis C. Whitman, Jr.
Telephone: 203-847-4558
Rooms: Ten, all with private bath.
Rates: $35 to $38, single; $55 to $65, double; continental breakfast included.
Facilities: Open all year. Closed Tuesdays from October to May. Lunch, dinner, bar. TV in parlor, six fireplaces in public rooms. All major credit cards accepted.

While close to everything, Silvermine Tavern still has a way of sweeping you worlds back in time. If you wish, you can stroll by the waterfall and feed ducks and swans on the millpond. The colonial crossroads village known as Silvermine has been swallowed up by the surrounding towns of Norwalk, Wilton, and New Canaan, but the Tavern still lies at the heart of a community of great Old World beauty.

This is one of the most popular dining places in the area, ☞ known for delicious New England traditional food. Thursday night is set aside for a fantastic buffet supper featuring steaks, fried chicken, and many salads, all of which you top off with a great array of desserts. Sunday buffet brunch features 20 different dishes.

Silvermine Tavern is furnished with old oriental rugs, antiques, old portraits, and great comfortable chairs and sofas surrounding huge fireplaces. The dining room overlooks the river and is decorated with over 1,000 antiques, primarily old farm tools and household artifacts.

In summer there is a ☛ brick-floored patio for al fresco dining. The guest rooms are comfortably furnished, many of them with old-fashioned tester beds.

Across the road from the Tavern you will find an authentic country store with a back room that is a museum of antique tools and gadgets. It also has a fine collection of Currier & Ives prints. Do take a leisurely drive around the back roads near the inn, too. They are a delight. Also in this area you have the well-known Silvermine Guild of Artists.

How to get there: From the Merritt Parkway take Exit 39 onto Route 7 south. Go south to the first traffic light and turn right onto Perry Avenue. In 2½ miles you'll find the inn at the intersection of Perry and Silvermine Avenues.

*I love all good inns, but secretly I have
a rather special fondness if the boniface is fat.*

Olive Metcalf

Bee and Thistle Inn
Old Lyme, Connecticut
06371

Innkeepers: Bob and Penny Nelson
Telephone: 203-434-1667
Rooms: Ten, eight with private bath.
Rates: $48 to $66, double occupancy, EP.
Facilities: Open all year. Closed Christmas Day. Breakfast.
Lunch and Dinner every day except Tuesdays. Sunday brunch, bar, lounge. American Express, MasterCard and Visa accepted.

This lovely old inn, built in 1756, sits on five and one-half acres bordering the Lieutenant River in historic Old Lyme, Connecticut. During summer the abundant flower gardens keep the inn filled to overflowing with color.

The guest rooms are all tastefully decorated. Your bed, maybe a four-poster or canopied, is covered with lovely old quilts or afghans.

There are six fireplaces in the inn. The one in the parlor is most inviting, a nice place for a cocktail or just good conversation. On Saturdays there is ☛ a harp player in here, and she is excellent.

☛ Breakfast in bed is a specialty of the inn. You will love it. ☛ Muffins, made each day, might be strawberry, rhubarb, or blackberry; freshly squeezed orange juice; plus almost anything you can think of. Lunch is so good, and dinner has some different touches, such as Stir-fried Scallops, and Scampi Pescatora. All entrees are accompanied by ☛ hot, homemade scones, honey, and butter. Delicious. The desserts have a uniqueness of their own; warm blueberry dumplings in heavy cream, to name but one.

This is a fine inn in a most interesting part of New England. You are in the heart of art, antiques, gourmet restaurants, and endless activities. Plan to spend a few days when you come.

And for your final pleasure there are two inn cats named Pepper and Wozzie. They are typical inn cats.

How to get there: Traveling north on I-95, take Exit 70 immediately on the west side of the bridge. At the bottom of the ramp, turn left. Take the first right at the traffic light, and turn left at the next light. The inn is the third house on your left. Traveling south on I-95, take Exit 70 and turn right at the bottom of the ramp. The inn is the third house on your left.

E: Big, thirsty towels, fresh flowers and ☛ a split of champagne to greet you. What a lovely inn.

olive Metcalf

Old Lyme Inn
Old Lyme, Connecticut
06371

Innkeeper: Diana Field Atwood
Telephone: 203-434-2600
Rooms: Five, all with private bath.
Rates: $45 to $50, continental breakfast included.
Facilities: Open all year. Closed Mondays. Lunch, dinner, bar.
    All major credit cards accepted.

The food here is  excellent and unusual. From the fresh soup stocks to the tender and flaky pastry shells, everything is homemade. The desserts are wonderful. The menu changes delightfully every three or four months. Some entrees I have tried and thoroughly enjoyed are Filet Mignon with a green peppercorn sauce, Quinelle of Halibut, and chicken served in cider with apples. They usually have a special of the day, and whatever it is, try it. You may gain a little weight, but you will enjoy yourself immensely.

Throughout the inn the chairs are blue velvet, luxuriously soft and comfortable. The large cocktail lounge has a bar that seats six, and a back bar the innkeeper found in

Philadelphia that is over 100 years old. This back bar has a beveled mirror that most museums would covet.

In addition to the two-level, lovely main dining room, there is a private room off the lobby for eight to 12 people, a really nice way to entertain good friends.

There is much to do in this area, with antique shops all over, the beautiful Connecticut River two minutes away, historic Essex just across the river, and a small, interesting museum called The Florence Griswold House almost directly across the street. Here you will get a fascinating glimpse of the art colony that flourished in Old Lyme at the beginning of the century.

How to get there: Traveling north on I-95, take Exit 70 immediately on the west side of the bridge. At the bottom of the ramp turn left. Take the first right at the traffic light, and turn left at the next light. The inn is on the right. Traveling south on I-95, take Exit 70. At the bottom of the ramp turn right. The inn is on the right.

E: *The bar is a real favorite spot of mine, with a bartender who remembers what you drink.*

> *Where else, in all good conscience,*
> *could I stay but at a country inn.*

The Elms
Ridgefield, Connecticut
06877

Innkeepers: Robert Scala and Violet Scala
Telephone: 203-438-2541
Rooms: 20, all with private bath, TV, and phone; some with
fireplace.
Rates: $55 to $90, double occupancy, EPB.
Facilities: Open all year. Closed Wednesdays and Christmas
Day. Lunch, dinner, Sunday brunch, bar. Piano enter-
tainment on Fridays, Saturdays, and at Sunday brunch.
All major credit cards accepted.

In 1760 a master cabinetmaker built this charming
Colonial house that is now known as The Elms. It is on a
historical site, for it was here that the Battle of Ridgefield was
fought during the Revolution. Since 1799, when the house
became an inn, the same loving care and artistry that marked
its beginning has been applied to every phase of its operation.

There is a 🖘 comfortable four-poster in one of the
quiet rooms upstairs. Another bedroom has maple spool
twin beds, and many of the rooms have their 🖘 own fire-

place. The quiet charm here induces slumber and assures the weary traveler of a restful night.

The brochure says, "To partake of a meal is no mundane experience in eating, but rather an adventure in dining." And so it is, with quail fresh from the fields, escargots flown fresh from France, and on and on, all of it delicious. The list of hors d'oeuvres is very impressive, with herring in cream, Scampi Romani, and smoked salmon but a few of the selections. There are five delicious soups, with the Onion au Gratin a specialty. Entrees like broiled English lamb chops with kidney and bacon, curry of sliced capon with wild rice and chutney, veal, steak, and rack of lamb are all on the menu. The dessert list is as long as the hors d'oeuvres list, with pears burgundy, tortonis, spumoni, and an old favorite of mine, zabaglione.

Ridgefield is a lovely town off the major highways. There are concerts in the park, tons of good shops to wander into, and good summer theater nearby.

How to get there: The inn is located at 500 Main Street in Ridgefield. From Route 7 take Route 35 right into town.

E: *Any place that serves* *Coupe Elizabeth has to get my nod. It is bing cherries bathed in cherry herring, sprinkled with cinnamon, and poured over vanilla ice cream. Yum. Yum.*

> *Man's cruelty to man knows almost no horizons.*
> *His continued existence, however, is justified*
> *when he says to a stranger, "Come in."*

olive Metcalf

Stonehenge
Ridgefield, Connecticut
06877

Innkeepers: David Davis and Douglas Seville
Telephone: 203-438-6511
Rooms: Eight, all with private bath and TV.
Rates: $58 to $70, tax included, double occupancy, EP.
Facilities: Open all year. Closed Tuesdays and New Year's Day.
Breakfast, lunch, dinner, bar. Parking. All major credit
cards accepted.

"You can't go home again," said Thomas Wolfe, but you
can go back to Stonehenge. David Davis and Douglas Seville
have been the innkeepers for several years and under their
direction, this beautiful country inn is blooming year round.
The setting is serenely beautiful, with the old white farmhouse overlooking the pond, which is bedecked with swans
and aflutter with Canada geese and ducks stopping in on
their migratory journeys. The Stonehenge Room, which was
once a porch, faces the pond and has a great view.

The chef, ☛ Jean-Maurice Calmels, is French-born
and trained, and nonpareil. The service, under the skilled

direction of Maitre d'Hotel Willie, is what I always dreamed it should be: deft, quiet, pleasant, and knowledgeable.

Address yourself seriously to the food. The appetizers are unusual, not to be skipped over lightly. The soups are poetic. The trout is live. "How long ago?" I asked. "About five minutes," was the reply. "The time it takes to come from the 'trout house.'"

The inventive touch with vegetables, the care taken with the sauces, all reflect the dedication with which M. Calmels approaches his task.

For a quiet dinner à deux, reserve a table in the bar. There, ☛ Len Gendal plays wonderful piano. He is excellent.

If you are tired of the "same old thing," book yourself into Stonehenge for a long weekend and find out what "haute cuisine" is all about. It is expensive, but worth every centime.

How to get there: The inn is 4½ miles from I-84. Take Route 7 to Ridgefield. Driving south from I-84, watch for the inn's small sign on the right.

෨

E: *My favorite room is the big one in the front of the main house. Any season, any weather, it is a home away from home with wine and cheese waiting and breakfast served on the spot.*

*Where else, in all good conscience,
could I stay but at a country inn.*

olive Metcalf

West Lane Inn
and
The Inn at Ridgefield
Ridgefield, Connecticut
06877

Innkeepers: Maureen Mayer and Henry Prieger
Telephone: West Lane 203-438-7323
      Ridgefield 203-438-8282
Rooms: 20, all with private bath, air conditioning, and TV;
    some with fireplace.
Rates: $75, single; $85 to $95, double; EPB.
Facilities: West Lane Inn open all year. The Inn at Ridgefield
    closed Mondays. Lunch, dinner, Sunday brunch, bar,
    lounge, piano nightly. American Express, MasterCard
    and Visa accepted.

Ridgefield is a lovely town, and we have a first here,
two totally separate inns next door to each other. West Lane
has the rooms, and The Inn at Ridgefield has the food.

West Lane's bedrooms are wonderfully spacious and
lovely, with magnificent decor. They are furnished with

comfortable chairs, either queen or king-sized beds, deluxe blankets, and huge, thirsty towels. There is a carved wood screen on the second floor you must not miss. West Lane does have a small dining room for breakfasts, and when you are ready for lunch or dinner you go across the driveway to The Inn at Ridgefield.

Chef Raymond Peron has a rather prestigious background, having been executive chef of the Hay-Adams Hotel in Washington, D.C., and of the S.S. *France*. He cooks superbly. There are seven or eight hors d'oeuvres, among them cold mussels in mustard sauce. A cold and a hot soup are served, and the entrees make my mouth water as I write. The Duck à l'Orange is a favorite, as is the Dover Sole. The inn special is a seafood platter served deliciously cold. Desserts, as expected, are grand, and a final touch are the special coffees.

Both inns are just around the corner from the famous Cannon Ball House, which was struck by a British fieldpiece during the Revolution. There are several museums in town, in addition to fine shops. You are also close to three summer theaters, Candlewood, Darien, and Westport.

How to get there: Coming north from New York on Route 684, or Route 7 from the Merritt Parkway, get off on Route 35 and follow it to Ridgefield. The inns are on Route 35 at the south end of town.

⧗

E: *The ends of* 🖝 *old, wooden wine and whiskey crates that line the porch of The Inn at Ridgefield let you know there are good things inside.*

Old Riverton Inn
Riverton, Connecticut
06065

Innkeepers: Pauline and Mark Telford
Telephone: 203-379-8678
Rooms: Ten, all with private bath.
Rates: $42 to $48, double occupancy, EPB.
Facilities: Open all year. Closed Mondays and Christmas Day.
  Lunch, dinner, bar. Dining room has wheelchair accessibility. All major credit cards accepted.

The village of Riverton was once called "Hitchcocksville," after the famous Hitchcock chairs which are still being manufactured in the old factory on the banks of the Farmington River, opposite the inn. The factory is open every day except Sunday until 5 p.m., and guests are always welcome.

Old Riverton Inn was originally opened in 1796. It was on the post road between Hartford and Albany, and was known as Ives Tavern. The inn was restored in 1937, and again in 1954. The 🖝 Grindstone Terrace was enclosed to make it available for year-round use. The floor of this room is made of grindstones which, according to 100-year-old records, were quarried in Nova Scotia, sent by ship to Long Island Sound, and then up the Connecticut River to Hartford. From there they were hauled by oxen to Collinsville, where they were used in the making of axes and machetes.

The Colonial dining room has low ceilings, Hitchcock chairs, excellent food, and home-baked breads and pastries. The Hobby Horse Bar has saddles for seats, and in charge of this charming room is a Philippine bartender who, like most of the help, has been here for years.

 Mints on the pillows at night is a very special touch I love. All of the rooms are cheerful, comfortable, and assure you of a good night's sleep. There is a lovely library area on the second floor that is a nice spot to relax in after looking at all of the things this charming village has to offer.

Antiques, galleries, a general store, the Hitchcock Museum, the Seth Thomas factory outlet, the Tartan Shop, Kitchen Shop, not to mention the Cat Nip Mouse Tearoom, are all here.

How to get there: The inn is 3½ miles from Winsted. Take Route 8 or Route 44 to Winsted. Turn east on Route 20, and it is approximately 1½ miles to the inn.

☀

E: *The drive on Route 20 between the inn and East Hartland or Granby is one of the most scenic in the state.*

The register of a country inn
is a treasure of the names of good people.

Under Mountain Inn
Salisbury, Connecticut
06068

Innkeepers: Lorraine and Albert Bard
Telephone: 203-435-0242
Rooms: Seven, all with private bath.
Rates: $52 to $59, double occupancy, continental breakfast
   included.
Facilities: Closed in March, Christmas Eve, and Christmas
   Day. Dining room closed Mondays and Tuesdays in
   winter. Dinner served Wednesday through Sunday.
   Sunday brunch, bar. No credit cards accepted.

The Bards looked long and hard at many country inns
before they found Under Mountain. They came east from
California, and the West Coast's loss is certainly our gain.
Under Mountain, in case you didn't know, is really an old
Colonial house. ☛ The bar was constructed from wide, old
boards hidden in the attic. Boards as wide as these were
made from trees known before the revolution as "king's
wood," which was reserved for the special use of His Majesty.
They certainly make a lovely bar.

The rooms are very well done, with antiques, comfortable beds, and ☛ bathrooms that are really knockouts. There is a library on the second floor so you can read away to your heart's content.

Though the house is old and Colonial and full of years, the food is slightly sophisticated with such delightful things as Escargots in Mushroom Caps, Steak au Poivre, poached salmon, and even sweetbreads. The soups and breads are homemade, absolutely delightful, and if you have room at the end, try an apple pancake. Sunday brunch is delightful. Come really early because the ☛ Clam Pie and Kippered Herring have a tendency to be all gone, they are so popular.

How to get there: Take Route 41 north 4½ miles from Salisbury. The inn is on the left. From New York state, take I-684 to Route 22, then Route 44 to Route 41.

🔔

E: *You know me and animals. Well, the inn cat is Pumpkin, and the dog is Sal.*

"Enough," he cried
and left with all speed
for the neighborhood inn.

olive Metcalf

Yankee Pedlar Inn
Torrington, Connecticut
06790

Innkeepers: Arthur and Gerald Rubens
Telephone: 203-489-9226
Rooms: 75, all have private bath, air conditioning, TV, sprink-
ler system, and smoke alarm.
Rates: $40, single; $50, double; EP. Package plans available
for off-season weekends.
Facilities: Open all year. Breakfast, lunch, dinner, bar, lounge.
All major credit cards accepted.

The Yankee Pedlar is a bit different from the other inns
in that it is an in-town inn. There were, at one time, many
such inns, but now only a few survive. Nice that this inn was
a survivor.

There is a wood sign in the dining room written by an
English minister, "Fate cannot harm me — I have dined well
to-day." And so will you as the food here is very good. One
specialty of the house is 🖝 Sauerbraten with Potato Pancakes, and, boy, do I love it. The veal you can cut with your
fork. All breads and desserts are prepared right here. The inn

has a beautiful silver serving cart now used to hold vintage wines. A nice way to present them.

All of the rooms are beautifully furnished with Hitchcock Colonial furniture. ☛ Dorothy Rubens is responsible for six new rooms, and they are lovely with hand-stencilled walls and fine furniture. Dorothy really has done an outstanding job. And one of the rooms has a fireplace. A beauty.

The lobby-living room has a large fireplace over which is mounted a pair of 1935 skis. They belonged to J. Franklin Ellis, the first ski instructor in the Mohawk ski area. The skis are not much, but he made them work.

There is much to do while visiting this inn. The Cornwall and Bull's covered bridges are nearby. You also have the Lime Rock races, but best of all is just driving around this beautiful section of country.

How to get there: From I-84 pick up Route 8 north at Waterbury. Take Route 8 to Exit 44 at Torrington. From Hartford, take Route 44 to Route 202 to Torrington. The inn is right in the center of town.

E: *The staff really tries to satisfy your every wish.*

Man has tendencies of many temperatures,
the warmest of which is hospitality.

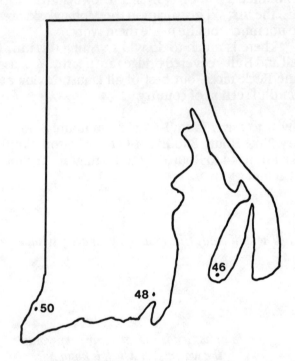

numbers on map refer to page numbers in this book

Rhode Island

Olive Metcalf

The Inn at Castle Hill
Newport, Rhode Island
02840

Innkeeper: Paul McEnroe; Jens Thillemann, general manager
Telephone: 401-849-3800
Rooms: 18, 14 with private bath.
Rates: $50 to $150, double occupancy, EPB.
Facilities: Inn open all year. Restaurant closed January
   through March, but breakfast served to house guests.
   Breakfast, lunch, and dinner served from May to No-
   vember. In November, December, and April, dinner
   served Thursday, Friday, and Saturday. Sunday brunch
   served from April through December. Bar. Live jazz on
   Sunday afternoons. Swimming from inn's private
   beach. MasterCard and Visa accepted.

The Inn at Castle Hill was built as a private home in
1874. Over the years it has undergone few changes, and the
warm atmosphere has been maintained. Thirty-two acres of
shoreline right on the entrance of Narragansett Bay offer a
natural setting for almost anything a person could desire.
The views from anyplace, in or about the inn, are breath-

takingly beautiful. The Atlantic Ocean and the bay are at your feet.

As for things to do, there is everything. Newport is the home of America's Cup Races, the Tennis Hall of Fame, and is famous for its great "cottages" lining the waterfront.

The inn has four dining rooms. The small one with only six tables, each set with different serving plates, is very special. Another is a light and airy oval room which, like the others, looks over the water. All of the food is prepared to order by a fine chef. Veal, beef, lamb, fowl, and seafood are prepared many ways and are beautifully served. Every day there are three homemade soups, together with an endless variety of appetizers.

The Tavern is a different room, with a beauty of a bar and a view unmatched, if you love the sea. There are Chinese teak and marble tables in the living areas, and the bannister on the staircase is its own delight.

Almost all the rooms are quite large and beautifully furnished. The paneling is magnificent, as are the oriental rugs that have been left here.

Innkeeper McEnroe has refurbished the entire inn with wallpapers that are color-coordinated with spreads and drapes, plus thick towels. Here the view outside is not enough for our innkeeper. He cares about the interior look, too.

How to get there: From the north take Route 138 into Newport, and follow Thames Street about 4½ miles to Ocean Drive. Look for the inn's sign on your right. From the west come across the Newport Bridge and take the scenic Newport Exit that goes onto Thames Street.

E: *The 10-mile ocean drive is among the most strikingly beautiful areas in New England.*

47

Olive Metcalf

Larchwood Inn
Wakefield, Rhode Island
02879

Innkeeper: Francis J. Browning
Telephone: 401-783-5454
Rooms: 15, eight with private bath.
Rates: $30, single, to $60, double; EP.
Facilities: Open all year. Restaurant, bar, cocktail lounge, formal gardens. Swimming, fishing, and skiing nearby. All major credit cards accepted.

Over the fireplace in the homey bar is carved "Fast by an Ingle Bleezing Finely," a quotation from the Scots' Robert Burns. ☞ His birthday, January 25th, is celebrated here, and last year a couple of pipers came over from Connecticut to help the party along. The Scottish flavor is all over this homelike country inn. The present innkeeper, Francis J. Browning, took over from his in-laws, the Camerons, who had been running things for the past quarter of a century. The Tam O'Shanter Cocktail Lounge serves up a delectable lunch each day except Sunday, and there are four other lovely rooms for dining or private entertaining.

Come summer there is a patio in the garden, where meals are served. The inn is situated in the heart of Rhode Island's beautiful South County. Saltwater beaches for bathing, fishing, and sunning are close by. In the winter it is only a short drive to Pine Top and Yawgoo Valley for skiing.

Rhode Island isn't all that big, you know, so it's never very far from anywhere to the Larchwood Inn.

How to get there: Take I-95 to Route 1. Exit from Route 1 at Pond Street, follow it to the end, and the inn will be immediately in front of you.

When you have but one night to spend
which inn to choose is as difficult
as the choice you had years ago
at the penny candy counter,
and equally rewarding.

Olive Metcalf

Shelter Harbor Inn
Westerly, Rhode Island
02891

Innkeepers: Jim and Debbye Dey
Telephone: 401-322-8883
Rooms: 18, all with private bath; one with fireplace.
Rates: $35 to $53, single; $40 to $60, double occupancy; EPB.
Facilities: Open all year. Breakfast, lunch, dinner, Sunday
    brunch, bar. Two paddle tennis courts with night light-
    ing. Swimming and summer theaters nearby. All major
    credit cards accepted.

If you would like a three-mile stretch of uncluttered
beach located just a few miles from a lovely, old country inn,
find your way to Rhode Island and the Shelter Harbor Inn.
Bring the children. There is a salt pond, too, often inhabited
by one of the inn dogs, Heidi, a friendly Newfoundland.

Eight of the guest rooms are in the restored farmhouse,
and ten more are located in the barn. There is a large central
living room here which opens onto a spacious deck, how
ideal for families. Or if your business group is small, have a
meeting right here.

The menu reflects the location of the inn, and at least half the items offered are from the sea. The Finnan Haddie is especially smoked in Narragansett. You can choose your place to eat, from the formal dining room to the more relaxed library. The sun porch has been turned into a pub bar. There is a delightful old wood stove to warm you, and Debbye's plants are everywhere. If weather permits, take a drink out to the secluded terrace.

If you can tear yourself from the beach, there is much to see around here. You are about halfway between Mystic and Newport. The ferry to Block Island leaves from Port Judith, takes an hour to cover the 12 miles, and when you arrive you will find it a super spot for bicycling. You can charter boats for fishing, or stand on the edge of the surf and cast your line into the sea. In the evenings there is Theater by the Sea in nearby Matunuck, or the Heritage Playhouse in Hopkinton.

How to get there: Take I-95 to Route 1. Follow Route 1 out of Westerly for about 5 miles. The inn is on the right side of the road when you're heading northeast.

E: *Authentic johnnycakes are served here. Delicious!*

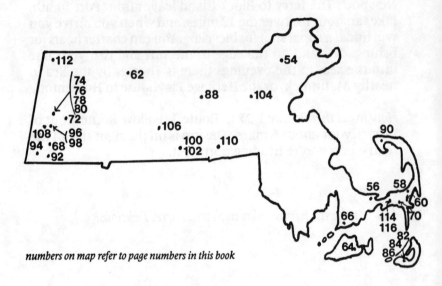

numbers on map refer to page numbers in this book

Massachusetts

Olive Metcalf

Andover Inn
Andover, Massachusetts
01810

Innkeepers: Henry Broekhoff and John Oudheusden
Telephone: 617-475-5903
Rooms: 33, 23 with private bath, some with running water;
all with air conditioning, TV, and phone. One suite.
Rates: $35 to $49, single; $45 to $59, double; $85, suite; EP.
Facilities: Closed last two weeks of August. Dining room
closed on Christmas. Breakfast, lunch, dinner, Sunday
brunch, bar. Accessible to wheelchairs. Elevator, bar-
bershop. All major credit cards accepted.

The inn is on the campus of Phillips Academy. You
expect ivy-covered buildings, and you get them in abundance. When you walk through the gracious front door of
the inn you are greeted by a wonderful living room with
fireplace.

The bar in the right corner of the main entrance room is
one of the coziest I have seen. ☛ The stools are overstuffed,
and so comfortable you hate to leave.

Rooms here have every modern convenience, includ-

54

ing color TV, radio, direct dial telephone, air conditioning, and full baths, all with a view of either the delightful inn gardens, the neighboring pond, or Phillips Academy.

The dining room is elegant, with crisp napery and crystal chandeliers. The chef, one of the owners, has a Dutch background, so the food is superb. Full breakfasts and ample lunches fit well with the broad dinner menus. And there is a special Sunday brunch from 11 to 2:45 p.m. Also on Sundays they have a special called Rijsttafel. It is an original Indonesian dish prepared the right way, and eaten in the proper manner. It consists of dry, steamed rice and an indefinite number of side dishes and sauces. The menu tells you how to eat this fabulous feast. It is served Sunday only, from 4 to 8:45 p.m., and is by reservation.

How to get there: The inn is 25 miles north of Boston on Route 28, near the intersection of Routes 93 and 495.

E: *Monday through Saturday evenings guests enjoy light classical music on the grand piano.*

*Modern man has done wondrous things
in preserving the whooping cranes
and country inns.*

Olive Metcalf

Cobb's Cove
Barnstable Village, Massachusetts
02630

Innkeeper: Evelyn Chester
Telephone: 617-362-9356
Rooms: Six suites, all with private bath.
Rates: $78 to $98, double occupancy, EPB.
Facilities: Closed mid-January to mid-February. Dinner available to house guests only. BYOB. No credit cards honored, but checks will be accepted.

The moment you walk in the door and are greeted by Evelyn and Henri-Jean, you know you have happened on a distinctive and delightful inn. You are taken to your suite, and what a marvelous view you have. ☛ The third-floor suite has the biggest skylight I have ever seen. It goes from almost the gable down to the eave. There is a couch in front of this skylight where you can sit, see all of Cape Cod Bay, Sandy Neck, and all the way to Provincetown Light. The other suites also have grand views, deliciously comfortable beds, and all the extras you expect at an extraordinary inn. The baths all have ☛ whirlpools, so relaxing after a day of travel. The soaps and bubble bath are pear-scented, a nice touch. Plenty of big towels and good, soft pillows.

The inn is on a very secluded and scenic piece of property. The bay is right at hand. The inn was built of 12 by 12-foot rough-cut timbers and many of the walls are done in rough burlap. The keeping room has a large Count Rumford shallow fireplace, comfortable chairs, and wonderful smells that come from Henri's kitchen. There is a terrace full of bird feeders made by Harry Holl of the Scargo Pottery. Harry also made many of the kitchen things Henri uses, including a huge salad bowl that is a rare beauty. In summer, breakfast is served on the terrace.

The dining room-library has a long hutch table that seats 14 quite comfortably. Dinner is served in three or five courses. The night I was there it started with 🐛 delicious mussels, then a special cauliflower dish done Henri's way. This was followed by a 🐛 fish (cod, I believe, and you can only believe because Henri reveals no kitchen information at all) so white and so tasty you wonder why you had ever eaten meat. Next came a salad, and finally a crème caramel for dessert, topped off by a great cup of 🐛 espresso coffee, a Henri specialty.

This is fine dining, and believe me, the innkeeper who joins you for every course is the reason this inn is such a success.

How to get there: Take Exit 6 off Route 6 (the main Cape highway) and go north on Route 6A. Turn right and go through the light in the middle of Barnstable Village. After you pass a church on your left, look for a sign saying "Cobb's Cove." Turn left and within 100 yards on your left you will see a driveway marked "Evelyn Chester." Take this drive to the inn.

E: *Vickey is the inn cat. He was given this name when he was very small and before anybody knew he was a male.*

Inn of the Golden Ox
Brewster, Massachusetts
02631

Innkeepers: Charles and Ruth Evans
Telephone: 617-896-3111
Rooms: Six, all share bathroom facilities.
Rates: $25 to $30, per room, EP.
Facilities: Open all year. During off season, dinner is served
Friday, Saturday, and Sunday. TV in lounge. Parking. No
credit cards accepted.

Housed in an 1828 building that was once a church, the
Inn of the Golden Ox is run by a man who used to be an
Episcopal minister, until he lost his voice. It is coming back,
and when you meet Charles Evans, half German, a quarter
Swiss, and a quarter Welsh, you feel that somehow, the right
thing has happened. A giant of a man, Mr. Evans welcomes
you to his inn.

The inn is small, and charmingly decorated with red-
and-white, checked tablecloths in one dining area, and
something more formal in the other. ☛ The menu, written
on blackboards, is German. Not all wurst and kraut, but truly

beautiful German cooking. There are six different schnitzels. Being a schnitzel lover, I have a difficult choice to make when I am here. Good German beer is available, as well as a nice selection of wine and cocktails.

The rooms for travelers are small, though they are clean and comfortable.

How to get there: Take Route 6A on the north side of Cape Cod to Brewster. The inn is at the intersection of 6A and Tubman Road.

⚖

E: Do not overlook the real innkeepers, Tylos, a black Labrador, and Bonnie, a cocker spaniel.

*The good morning greeting and the
good night good wish can only be found in a country inn.*

The Town House Inn
Chatham, Massachusetts
02633

Innkeepers: Russell and Svea Peterson
Telephone: 617-945-2180
Rooms: 20, all with private bath, TV, refrigerator, and phone;
two have water beds; one cottage with fireplace.
Rates: $60 to $75, double occupancy, continental breakfast
included.
Facilities: Open all year. Breakfast only meal served. Friday
night band concerts. Near restaurants, golf, tennis, and
beaches. All major credit cards accepted.

The front porch that overlooks Main Street beckons
me. The 4th of July parade, one of the summer's biggest
events, goes right by the front door. Best seat in town is the
porch of this inn.

The original structure dates back to the 1820s. Remains
of the foundation can still be seen in the cellar, and some of
the original woodwork is still here. The carved moldings and
wood trim depict harpoon and oar motifs. The floors are
made of hemlock, and the original walls, recently exposed,

have hand-painted scrolling.

The rooms are immaculate; matter of fact, the whole inn is. If you have always wanted to try a water bed, here is your chance. I think they are neat. The rest of the beds are very comfortable, also. All of the linens and towels are laundered right here by Svea. She likes to hang them out, when weather permits, for that lovely smell of fresh air.

Breakfast is the only meal served here, but it is special. Russ bakes the muffins and Svea bakes some delicious Scandinavian goodies. Restaurants, shops, churches, beaches, a golf course, tennis courts, and the library are all within walking distance of the inn. A fishing pier recently was built near here. Party boats are for hire.

The three Peterson children are no longer small, but they still help run the inn.

How to get there: Take Route 6 (mid-Cape highway) to Exit 11, Route 137 south to Route 28 and east to the center of downtown Chatham. Watch for the Eldredge Library on your left. The inn is next door.

E: *Russ is rightfully proud of his cooking.*

How good of you to have asked me in.

Deerfield Inn
Deerfield, Massachusetts
01342

Innkeeper: Paul J. Burns
Telephone: 413-774-5587
Rooms: 23, all with private bath and air conditioning.
Rates: $65 and $70, single or double occupancy, EP.
Facilities: Open all year. Closed Christmas Day. Breakfast, lunch, dinner. Cocktail lounge, two bars. Elevator. Color TV in lounge. Museum, Deerfield Academy, historic house tours nearby. All major credit cards accepted.

A few years back a serious fire did extensive damage to this lovely old inn, but alumni of Deerfield and many others banded together and rebuilt the inn. They did such an exquisite job the Federal government has designated the inn a ☛ National Historic Site.

☛ The rocking chairs on the front porch somehow let you know how lovely things will be inside. The parlors are beautifully furnished with mostly twentieth century copies or adaptations. The Beehive Parlor, done in shades of blue, is a restful place for a cocktail or two. The main dining room is spacious, serving the kind of food befitting the setting. The chef prepares a daily special, taking advantage of seasonal and local market offerings. He also does magic things with veal, chicken, and fish.

The luncheon menu has some interesting and quite different offerings, such as Lamb Brochette, marinated lamb with vegetables on a skewer, and very good. There is also Chicken Mandarin Salad that will light up your day. By the way, all the baking is done right here.

The bedrooms are joys, Beauty-Rest mattresses, matching bedspreads and drapes, comfortable chairs, and good lights for restful reading or needlework. The baths have been color-coordinated with the rooms they serve. Little to nothing has been left to chance in this restoration.

There is a coffee shop on the lower level, which gives off onto an outdoor garden. Perfect spot for informal meals, and a place the children will love.

How to get there: From I-91 take Exit 24 northbound. Go 6 miles north on Route 5. At the sign for Old Deerfield Village take a left. The inn will be on your left just past the Academy.

E: *For an old "inn creeper" like me this inn is the icing on the cake.*

The good morning greeting and the good night good wish can only be found in a country inn.

The Charlotte Inn
Edgartown, Massachusetts
02539

Innkeepers: Gery and Paula Conover
Telephone: 617-627-4751
Rooms: 18, 16 with private bath; some with fireplace.
Rates: In season, $75 to $175; off season, $28 to $125; double
　　occupancy; continental breakfast included Monday
　　through Saturday.
Facilities: Open all year. In season, lunch and dinner. Off
　　season, dinner on weekends. Sunday brunch year
　　round. Reservations a must. Gift shop and gallery. Sail-
　　ing, swimming, fishing, golf, and tennis nearby. Master-
　　Card and Visa accepted.

　　The start of your vacation is a 45-minute ferry ride to
Martha's Vineyard. It's wise to make early reservations for
your automobile on the ferry. There are also cabs if you
prefer not to take your car.
　　When you open the door to the inn you are in the
☛ Edgartown Art Gallery, with interesting artifacts and
paintings, both watercolor and oil. This is a well-appointed

gallery featuring such artists as Ray Ellis who has a fine talent in both media. The inn also has an unusual gift shop.

Food here is French. The restaurant, called Chez Pierre, is small and intimate with many artifacts, plants, unusual windows, and oh, the food! The hors d'oeuvres are unlike any you have ever had, such as sliced smoked Nantucket pheasant, or fresh seafood marinated in a combination of lemon and lime juices. There are more of these goodies. The entrees change with the seasons. Just a few are ☛ Broiled Swordfish with Caviar, Poached Fillet of Whitefish with Spinach Cream Sauce, and the list goes on, one better than the next. Desserts I will let you discover, and I do not want to meet your diet doctor.

Sunday brunch is worth the trip alone, ☛ freshly squeezed orange juice, Salt-cured Salmon with Dill sauce, freshly baked croissants. Heaven!

The rooms are authentic. There are early American four-poster beds, fireplaces, and the carriage house is sumptuous. The second-floor suite with fireplace I could live in. Paula has a touch with rooms, comfortable furniture, ☛ down pillows, ☛ down comforters, and all the amenities. As an example, the shower curtains are eyelet and so pretty. As a finishing touch, there are plenty of large towels.

Across the street is the Garden House, and it is Edgartown at its best. Paula, by the way, has green hands, and all about are gardens that just outdo each other.

How to get there: Reservations are a must if you take your car on the ferry from Woods Hole, Massachusetts. Forty-five minutes later you are in Vineyard Haven. After a 15-minute ride, you are in Edgartown, and on Summer Street is the inn.

E: *Gery and Paula are special innkeepers, but they do need the help of Kim the dog and Charlotte the cat.*

Coonamessett Inn
Falmouth, Massachusetts
02541

Innkeeper: Joe Badot
Telephone: 617-548-2300
Rooms: Three, two with private bath; 22 cottage suites.
Rates: $23 to $85, per room, EP.
Facilities: Open all year. Breakfast, lunch, dinner, bar. Parking. All major credit cards accepted.

In 1796, in a rolling field that sloped gently down to a lovely pond, Mr. Thomas Jones constructed a house and barn that was to become Coonamessett Inn (Indian, for "the place of the large fish"). The framework of the house is finished with wooden peg joints, and much of the interior paneling is original. Many of the bricks in the old fireplaces are thought to be made of ballast brought from Europe in the holds of sailing ships.

Don't despair if you can't get a room in the inn itself. ☛ The cottage suites are fine, and especially good if you are traveling en masse, with the family. The grounds are beautiful and are kept in mint condition year round. I love the Cape off season, and it is good to know that no matter what day I decide to come, I will receive a cordial welcome here.

The food is excellent, offered from a large, varied menu, and served by friendly waitresses. Breakfasts are memorable. Lunch attracts a large group, for this place is really well known. And dinner is great, with lobster served four different ways. You can even have lobster sauce on your scrod. Meat eaters are not forgotten either; two favorites are featured, sweetbreads and bacon with sauce supreme, and a lamb chop mixed grill. ☛ Desserts have a menu all their own. Fantastic.

There are little shops to lure you, and all around you will see the loveliest array of grass, trees, flowers, shrubs . . . and peace. Don't forget the peace.

How to get there: Take Route 28 at the bridge over the canal, and go into Falmouth. Turn left on Jones Road, and at the intersection of Gifford Street you will see the inn.

E: *I wish I lived closer, because I like the whole thing, starting with the flower arrangements, fresh every other day, that are done by a man who really knows how to arrange.*

*The chill of a wood-stove-warmed bedroom
evaporates in the crisp smell of bacon for breakfast.*

olive Metcalf

Windflower Inn
Great Barrington, Massachusetts
01230

Innkeepers: Barbara and Gerald Liebert, Claudia and John
    Ryan
Telephone: 413-528-2720
Rooms: 12, all with private bath, many with fireplace.
Rates: $55 per person, double occupancy, MAP.
Facilities: Open all year. Breakfast, dinner, full license. Res-
    ervations a must. Pool. Golf, tennis, downhill and cross-
    country skiing, music, and theater nearby. No credit
    cards honored, but personal checks accepted.

Barbara and Claudia, mother and daughter, are the
chefs in this lovely inn. They give you a choice of three
entrees each evening, and all are cooked fresh. The summer
vegetable garden is a 50 by 90-foot spread of delights. I am
sure a lot of the produce is preserved for winter use. The
breads, pies, muffins, and cakes are all ☛ homemade. The
dining room features Currier and Ives snow scenes on the
walls and a ☛ coffeepot bubbling on the mantel all day.
Late afternoon you have your choice of tea or cocktail with a

great assortment of hors d'oeuvres.

The rooms are spacious, and all the beds are new. All rooms have private baths, and many have fireplaces.

A game room offers choices of chess, cribbage, backgammon, Scrabble, and jigsaw puzzles. The living room, full of good early American antiques, is comfortable.

The inn animals are Tawny, a yellow Lab, and Libby, a beautiful Springer spaniel.

There is so much to do in this area it is hard to recount it all. Golf is across the street. The inn's own pool is very relaxing, and in summer you have Tanglewood, Jacob's Pillow, and the Berkshire Theater nearby.

How to get there: The inn is on Route 23, 3 miles west of Great Barrington.

E: *Gerald moved his grandmother's kitchen table down here from the Tulip Tree Inn in Vermont that they owned. He kneads his good French bread on it.*

> *Our sympathy for the hardships*
> *of our forbears should be somewhat mitigated*
> *by the fact that they had the best*
> *of country inns.*

Country Inn
Harwichport, Massachusetts
02646

Innkeepers: David and Kathleen Van Gelder
Telephone: 617-432-2769
Rooms: Seven, all with private bath.
Rates: $45 to $50, double occupancy, $5 per room breakfast
credit included.
Facilities: Open all year. Dinner by reservation. Lounge, bar,
and private dining room for small parties. Tennis, swim-
ming pool. Ocean beach privileges. MasterCard and
Visa accepted.

The Country Inn is what its name implies, a lovely old
Cape home on six acres, covered with rambling roses. Centrally located on the Cape, it makes a great home base for
exploring this wonderful part of the world, with its excellent
shopping for just about everything.

The dining room is open to the public for dinner and
offers a varied menu, from French and Italian dishes to the
more traditional New England fare. All meals include absolutely delicious ☛ homemade cranberry, lemon, and

pumpkin breads. Fish specials include escalloped oysters baked in heavy cream, and ocean-fresh haddock, baked, or baked and stuffed. From fish you can turn to Chicken Cape Cod with ☛ cranberry-spice glaze, Chicken Cordon Bleu, or Filet Mignon. The perfect ending is homemade Apple Crumb Pie with homemade Cinnamon Ice Cream. To make your meal complete they have a choice of five unusually spirited coffees.

Breakfasts are special fun. The normal eggs and omelets are all done differently, which, with the inn's homemade breads, make the whole meal a delight. The inn has 11 fireplaces. Three are in use downstairs. The rest are in the bedrooms and are lovely to look at, but unfortunately cannot be used.

The innkeeper has recently acquired a boat and his captain's license. For a modest fee, he will take house guests on day trips to Monomoy (part of the National Seashore) for birdwatching, picnicking, and swimming. The fee includes your picnic lunch.

How to get there: Take Route 6 to Exit 10. Go right on Route 124 and continue to a stop sign, about 2 miles away. Take a right on Route 39, and in one mile the inn will be on your right.

ᛞ

E: *The inn was once the guest house on the estate of one of the founders of the Jordan Marsh Company.*

The time between sunset and the completeness of night
should be spent around a well-laid board
with assurances of a warm bed to follow.

The Morgan House
Lee, Massachusetts
01238

Innkeepers: Beth and Bill Orford
Telephone: 413-243-0181
Rooms: 11, all share baths.
Rates: $25 to $60, double occupancy, EPB.
Facilities: Open all year. Lunch, dinner, bar, lounge. Game room. American Express, MasterCard, and Visa accepted.

The Morgan House is another of my few in-town inns. Very nice to have in any town. The inn has a long and interesting history dating back to 1826 when it was built as a private home. In 1853 it was converted into a stagecoach inn, and an inn it has remained.

The lobby is papered in ☞ old registration sheets, many of them showing the names of the noted visitors over the past 100 years, such as Ulysses S. Grant, Robert E. Lee, Buffalo ''Bill'' Cody, Horace Greeley, and George Bernard Shaw. Many of the pages are beautifully decorated in flowing script advertising the bill at the local opera house.

The guest rooms are furnished with early American

pieces. The walls are stencilled, and everything is clean and crisp. There is a porch on the second floor looking over Main Street for the guests' use. Wicker chairs make an afternoon here extremely delightful. The inn also has a fully equipped game room for your relaxation.

Now for the best part, the food. ☛ The veal is butchered and pounded here in the inn's kitchen. You just know it will be good. The menu shows 13 different appetizers to go with the entrees, every one of which is prepared here. One different entree you should try is the Yankee Pork Chops, two generously cut chops served with a dressing of apples and raisins. All breads and desserts are created in the kitchen. An example is Pear Helen, ice cream capped with half a pear, laced with chocolate sauce, and topped with a dab of sweet whipped cream.

You can host a small meeting or special occasion in the Coach Room on the second floor. The room can accommodate 50 people.

There is so much to do in this lovely part of the world I just may write a book on the subject.

How to get there: From the Massachusetts Turnpike, take Exit 2. Follow Route 20 west one mile to the center of Lee. The inn will be on your left.

E: *The ☛ square antique grand piano in the bar was made by the G.A. Miller Company of Boston and is a rare beauty.*

olive Metcalf

The Candle Light Inn
Lenox, Massachusetts
01240

Innkeepers: Lynne and James DeMayo
Telephone: 413-637-1555
Rooms: Four rooms, all with private bath; three suites.
Rates: $45 to $75, double occupancy; $85 to $125, suite; EP.
Facilities: Open all year. Lunch, afternoon tea, dinner Fridays
and Saturdays. Lounge and Village Tavern. Entertain-
ment on weekends. All major credit cards accepted.

Christmas is a time of royal splendor here at the inn.
They 👉 decorate for each season, but Christmas is just
something special and worth a trip from anywhere.

An old wagon and an old double sled are on the lawn,
Tiffany lamps are on the porch, and a lovely flower cart is in
the entrance hall. Straight ahead is the bar, and what a bar,
done pub-style with some of the 👉 greatest stemware I
have ever seen.

The dessert cart sits at the entrance of one of the dining
rooms with a beautiful array of all 👉 homemade desserts,
each one better than the next. There is a gracious fireplace in

this dining room. Napery is bluest white. The chairs are comfortable, and the food divine. All the food is fresh and cooked to order; nothing frozen in this chef's kitchen except the ice cubes. The hors d'oeuvres list is more than ample, with four different kinds of clams, shrimp, and oysters, in addition to my favorite, garlicky escargots.

Entrees are interesting. At lunch do try the Chicken Pot Pie. It is deliciously different. Dinner entrees like Shrimp, Crabmeat and Scallops Mornay en Casserole are a delight. Stuffed crepes, or one of the chicken dishes, tempt me to try eating everything on the menu.

The chef-owner, Jim, cooks only with copper utensils, and the food is even served from copper. ☞ Fresh strawberries are served here almost every month of the year.

Flowers are all over the inn, with Boston ferns at the windows, and fuchsias in abundance, usually hanging together with impatiens. And the backyard in summer is a wealth of blooms.

How to get there: The inn is at 53 Walker Street. Turn into Lenox on Route 7-A, off Route 7.

Ⴘ

E: *The small bar with the gleaming stemware is just a great way to end a day.*

Man has tendencies of many temperatures, the warmest of which is hospitality.

The Gateways Inn
Lenox, Massachusetts
01240

Innkeepers: Lilliane and Gerhard Schmid
Telephone: 413-637-2532
Rooms: 8, all with private bath; one suite with fireplace.
Rates: $45 to $65, double; $85 to $125, suite; continental
    breakfast included.
Facilities: Open all year. Restaurant closed Sundays and Mon-
    days in winter. In summer, dinner by reservation only.
    Free guest privileges at Haus Andreas. MasterCard and
    Visa accepted.

The Gateways began as a mansion built for Harley
Proctor of Proctor and Gamble, the Ivory soap magnate. It is
in the shape of his favorite product, a cake of soap. It is square
and flat on top.

Chef-owner Gerhard was the winner of both ☛ a silver and a gold medal in the 1968 International Culinary
Competition, and ☛ three Olympic gold medals in 1976.
Gerhard also had the honor of preparing Boston's royal
luncheon for Queen Elizabeth during her bicentennial visit

in 1976. To add to the laurels, the Gateways rates four stars in the Mobil Guide. There is really not much more I can say about the food. It is just superb.

Two bedrooms, with their high ceilings, are perfect for the massive furniture with which they are furnished. The other bedrooms, equally lovely, have Colonial-style furniture. Color-coordinated towels add just the right final touch. The suite is called the Fiedler Suite because Arthur Fiedler stayed in it so many times. It is lavish in its appointments, and worth all it costs to spend a night in.

The sister inn, Haus Andreas, is named for the Schmid's son, and is but five miles away. It is a lovely, old Colonial mansion with a charming pastoral view. Here you will have complimentary guest privileges entitling you to swim, play tennis, and ride bicycles.

How to get there: Take Route 7 to Route 7A. The inn is on Route 7A, one block away from the intersection of Routes 183 and 7A.

E: *The oval windows beside the front door and the magnificent stairway alone are worth a visit here.*

*The time between sunset and the completeness of night
should be spent around a well laid board
with assurances of a warm bed to follow.*

The Village Inn
Lenox, Massachusetts
01240

Innkeepers: Clifford Rudisill and Ray Wilson
Telephone: 413-637-0020
Rooms: 27, eight with private bath.
Rates: $40 to $90, double occupancy, EP.
Facilities: Open all year. Breakfast, lunch, afternoon tea. Lounge and pub. During July and August a special after-concert menu. MasterCard and Visa accepted.

There is a saying here at the inn, "If you can't be a house guest in the Berkshires, be ours." This surely would be a fine choice. The rooms are so clean and cheerful. The inn's walls are done in Colonial-style wallpaper of the very best selection. One long hall upstairs has  photographs of our presidents. A nice touch.

The Village Tavern was built in the old cellars, and is furnished with seats made from church pews. On those blustery winter days there is a cheery fire to go with your drink.

The inn has a  lounge, bar, and a comfortable living room. In here are changing art shows. A nice idea.

A real first is an authentic English tea served from 3:30 to 5:00 with scones, pastries, and small tea sandwiches. To make it perfect, you are provided with Devonshire cream (clotted, double cream).

Breakfast is a thing of joy. Any inn that serves eggs Benedict with a glass of champagne gets my hearty applause. Another clap of the hands goes for their Irish coffee. In addition to breakfast, there are many good things to eat. Overstuffed sandwiches, great salads, unusual quiches are but a few of the luncheon specialties.

The inn is near churches, shops, the library, and the bus stop.

How to get there: Take Route 7-A off Route 7 and turn on Church Street in Lenox. The inn is on the right.

𝒳

E: *A piano and an organ at your disposal in the living room is very nice.*

> *Modern man has done wonderous things*
> *in preserving the whooping cranes*
> *and country inns.*

olive Metcalf

Wheatleigh
Lenox, Massachusetts
01240

Innkeepers: Susan and Linfield Simon
Telephone: 413-637-0610
Rooms: 16, all with private bath.
Rates: $85 to $250, double occupancy, continental breakfast included.
Facilities: Open all year. Breakfast, dinner served Tuesday through Sunday, bar, lounge. Swimming, tennis, and cross-country skiing on premises. No credit cards accepted at the inn; Diners Club, MasterCard, and Visa accepted at the restaurant.

In the heart of the beautiful Berkshires, overlooking a lake, amid lawns and gardens on 22 self-contained acres stands the estate of Wheatleigh, former home of the Countess de Heredia. The centerpiece of these 22 acres is an elegant private palace fashioned after an Italian palazzo. The cream-colored manse recreates the architecture of sixteenth-century Florence. You must read the brochure of Wheatleigh, for it says it all so well.

Patios, pergolas, porticos, and terraces surround this lovely old mansion. The carvings over the fireplaces, ☞ cupids entwined in garlands, are exquisite. In charming contrast, the inn also has the ☞ largest collection of contemporary ceramics in the New England area. There are many lovely porcelain pieces on the walls.

The bar-lounge, with bookcases lining the walls, a piano, and a great collection of records make a drink rather special.

And imagine a ☞ great hall with a grand staircase right out of a castle in Europe. There also are exquisite stained glass windows in pale pastels, plus gorgeous, comfortable furniture. From the great hall you can hear the tinkle of the fountain out in the garden.

The rooms are ☞ smashing with lots of white dotted swiss and eyelet material for the canopy beds. Do you long for your own balcony overlooking a lovely lake? No problem. Reserve one here.

One dines by candlelight in the Victorian dining room on such things as Shrimp Mario, sauteed jumbo shrimp served with their own special wine sauce. Lamb chops ☞ one and one-half-inches thick are perfection. A wonderfully complete wine list caps any meal here.

How to get there: From Stockbridge at the Red Lion Inn where Route 7 turns right, go straight on Prospect Hill Road, bearing left. Go past the Stockbridge Bowl and up a hill to Wheatleigh. From the Massachusetts Turnpike, take Exit 2, and follow signs to Lenox. In the center of Lenox, take Route 183, pass the main gate of Tanglewood, and then take the first left on West Hawthorne. Go one mile to Wheatleigh.

E: *The inn dog is Bailey, a lovely golden retriever, and the cats are Moon Shadow and Mariah.*

The Four Chimneys Inn
Nantucket, Massachusetts
02554

Innkeepers: Anthony and Betty Gaeta
Telephone: 617-228-1912
Rooms: 12, ten with private bath.
Rates: $70 to $130, double occupancy, continental breakfast
　　included.
Facilities: Closed mid-December to Daffodil Festival. Conti-
　　nental breakfast only meal served. BYOB. American
　　Express, MasterCard, and Visa accepted.

　　The inn is on famous Orange Street where 126 sea
captains built their mansions. It was constructed circa 1835
by Captain Frederick Gardner. In 1856 Freeman Adams purchased this home and converted it into "The Bay View
House." The house had a motto by Mr. Adams: "No pains will
be spared to insure the comforts of its patrons." This feeling is
being carried out by the present owners who have done an
excellent restoration job.
　　All the rooms have been decorated with unbelievable
period furnishings. One of the bedrooms has a four-poster,

canopy bed and a huge armoire that beggars description. Many other rooms have canopy beds, and one room has its own porch. The third floor of the inn has marvelous views of the sea and the quaint rooftops of Nantucket town.

There is a grand staircase to the second floor. It does not take much imagination to envision beautifully gowned ladies floating down to join you.

The sitting rooms have fireplaces, and you have the use of the game table, cable television, and piano.

Continental breakfast, the only meal served here, always includes some unusual muffins which are excellent. In the late afternoon hors d'oeuvres are served to go along with your drinks. The inn has an extensive collection of menus from area restaurants to help you choose a spot for your lunch or dinner.

How to get there: Go up Main Street to the bookstore on your left. This is Orange Street where you turn left. The inn will be on your left.

E: The antique Chinese rugs are what you dream the old ship captains brought back with them.

> When you have but one night to spend
> which inn to choose is as difficult
> as the choice you had years ago
> at the penny candy counter,
> and equally rewarding.

Olive Metcalf

Jared Coffin House
Nantucket, Massachusetts
02554

Innkeepers: Philip and Margaret Read
Telephone: 617-228-2400
Rooms: 58; nine in main house; 16 simpler rooms in Eben
Allen Wing; three rooms in Swain house, connected to
the Eben Allen Wing; 12 rooms in Daniel Webster house
across the patio; 18 rooms in two houses across the
street.
Rates: $35, single; $65 to $100, double; EP.
Facilities: Open all year. Breakfast, lunch, dinner, taproom.
Eben Allen Room for private parties. Near swimming
and tennis. All major credit cards accepted.

It is well worth the thirty-mile trip by ferry, or the plane
trip from Boston or New York, to end up at the Jared Coffin
House. Built as a private home in 1845, the three-story brick
house with slate roof became an inn only 12 years later. The
inn passed through many hands before it came to the extremely 🖘 capable ones of Philip and Margaret Read.
The public rooms at the inn reflect charm and warmth.

The furnishings are Chippendale and Sheraton, and showing the results of the world-wide voyaging by the Nantucket whalemen are Chinese and Japanese objet's d'art and furniture.

To add to the charm are many fabrics and some furniture that have been made right here on the island. In addition to the main house, there are several other close-by houses that go with the inn. All are done beautifully for your every comfort.

☛ The taproom, located on the lowest level, is a warm, happy, fun place. Here you meet the local people and spin yarns with all. Old pine walls and hand-hewn beams reflect a warm atmosphere. Luncheon is served down here with good burgers and great, hearty soups. During the winter this is a nice spot for informal dinners.

The main dining room, ☛ papered with authentic wallpapers, is quiet and elegant. Wedgewood china and pistol-handled silverware make dining a special pleasure, and reflect the good life demanded by the nineteenth-century owners of the great Nantucket whaling ships.

The inn is located in the heart of Nantucket's Historic District, about one-eighth mile from a public beach, and one mile from the *largest* public beach and tennis courts. It's a pleasant three-mile bicycle ride from superb surf swimming on the South Shore.

How to get there: To get to Nantucket, take a ferry from Hyannis (April through January) or Woods Hole (January through March and summer months). First call 617-540-2022 for reservations. Or take a plane from Boston, Hyannis, or New York. The House is located 2 blocks north of Main Street, and 2 blocks west of Steamboat Wharf.

🐧

E: *The size and the quantity of the luxurious bath towels pleased me greatly. The housekeeping staff does a wonderful job, and the exquisite antiques reflect their loving care.*

Olive Metcalf

Ships Inn
Nantucket, Massachusetts
02554

Innkeepers: John and Bar Krebs; Lynne Keagy, Manager
Telephone: 617-228-0040
Rooms: 12, ten with private bath.
Rates: $25 to $35, single; $55 to $70, double; continental
   breakfast included from June 15 to October 31.
Facilities: Closed after Thanksgiving to Easter. Dinner every
   day except Tuesday, bar, lounge. American Express,
   MasterCard, and Visa accepted.

A plaque outside this inn reads: "Site of the birthplace
of Lucretia Coffin Mott 1793–1880. First woman abolitionist
and advocate of woman suffrage."

The inn's location provides a quiet spot, yet it is close,
indeed within easy walking distance, to the shops, theaters,
restaurants, and historic sites of the village.

Food here is served in a dining room called 🖝 The
Captain's Table, and were he still about, he would be proud
of the good vittles that come from the kitchen. I had the Veal
Scallops on one occasion. They were sauteed in butter, garlic,

lemon, and parsley, and they were excellent. All sorts of fresh fish, creatively prepared, are offered along with lamb and steaks. The desserts are sinful, but then, aren't they all.

The Dory Bar and Lounge is watched over by Bradshaw, who by his own admission is the best bartender and worst liars' poker player on the island. This is a very relaxed spot for cocktails before your good dinner. And if you wish to be just a bit active, a dart board and several backgammon boards are provided for your entertainment.

The rooms are correctly comfortable with twin or double beds and decorated as you would expect here on the island of Nantucket, a favorite place of mine.

How to get there: Go up Main Street past the bookstore on your left to Fair Street. Turn left and you will find the inn on your right.

E: *The plants in the dining room add a lot of warmth to The Captain's Table.*

Snug in a country inn, I have finally found the perfect topping to a windy Cape Cod day.

olive Metcalf

Country Inn at Princeton
Princeton, Massachusetts
01541

Innkeepers: Don and Maxine Plumridge
Telephone: 617-464-2030
Rooms: Six suites, all with private bath.
Rates: $95, double occupancy, continental breakfast included.
Facilities: Open all year. Closed Mondays and Tuesdays. Dinner served Wednesday through Sunday. Sunday brunch. American Express, MasterCard, and Visa accepted.

"The year 1890 had a way about it," says this inn's brochure, and it is so right. The inn is a 🐄 Victorian delight. It was built with meticulous attention to every detail by Charles G. Washburn, an industrialist and outspoken senator, and a close friend of Theodore Roosevelt.

The parlor is exquisite with original, slowly whirling, Casa Blanca ceiling fans, plus Victorian chairs and couches that are beautifully upholstered and very comfortable. All through the inn you will find 🐄 greenery displayed with fine taste.

There are three elegant dining rooms. The Red Room is a private party spot for up to 12 people. There is the Garden Room; there's also the main dining room, with five Casa Blanca fans on its ceiling. From the gracious windows you have a distant view of Boston's twinkling lights at night.

Cuisine is continental French and excellent. The menu changes every six weeks. Don and Maxine have put their good business experience to work by finding two chefs worthy of their aims to create an inn with the best food in New England. Chris Woodward is the head chef and Wayne Gorenson is the second. Together they make magic. One of the entrees I had was ☛ Salmon en Croute, fresh filets stuffed with a mousse of tender scallops and watercress, all wrapped in puff pastry and served with a butter sauce and lemon. Do try it.

The accommodations are six extremely ☛ spacious parlor suites. They are sumptuous. Each one is different, and I could live forever in any one of them.

How to get there: From just north of Worcester on Route 290 take Route 140 north to Route 62, and turn left to Princeton. When you reach the blinker by the post office turn right, and the inn is on your right just up the hill.

⌛

E: *By now you all know I am an animal nut, and so are Don and Maxine. Reno is a Doberman, and a real pussy cat. Crystal is a magnificent Umbrella Cockatoo, Goose is the Cockatiel, and Poncho is a yellow-naped Amazon parrot.*

Olive Metcalf

Oceans Inn
Provincetown, Massachusetts
02657

Innkeepers: Mark Cross and Horace Stowman
Telephone: 617-487-0358
Rooms: 16, ten with private bath, the rest with running water.
Rates: $30 to $60, double occupancy, EP.
Facilities: Inn closed late November to April 1. Bar and restaurant open all year. Brunch, dinner. American Express, MasterCard, and Visa accepted.

The bar and lounge are the inn's answer to Sardi's. The walls are covered with autographed photographs of Provincetown's wide family of performing artists. The bar itself is fun, and interesting drinks are served. Brandy snifters of either 12 or 22-ounce capacity are used for an array of about ☛ 35 to 40 different frozen fruit drinks. All the glassware used is in excellent taste. Someone has taken the time to do it right. I think it makes a drink taste much better to be in exactly the right glass.

The dining room is decorated with original etchings by ☛ Al Hirschfeld, the *New York Times* theater section illustrator. The menu covers are also done by him, and they are creative and excellent. He does not do the food, however, but a great chef does. Whether it is brunch or dinner, it is delicious.

Brunch and dinner, weather permitting, are served on the garden patio and on the deck overlooking famous, old Provincetown Harbor. In summer every Friday afternoon different artists display their work in the patio garden. Rain date is Sunday. The art and the food combine to make a wonderful experience.

The inn is old and comfortably furnished with wicker chairs and either king-sized or double beds. On the third floor are two rooms with expansive views of the harbor.

It is hard to list all there is to do out here in Provincetown, theater, arts, shops, but just walk out of the inn and turn right. You will find more than enough.

How to get there: Take Route 6 (Mid-Cape Highway) all the way out to Provincetown. The inn is at 386A Commercial Street (the main street of town).

E: *Over the bar is this sign: "May the roof above us never fall in, and we friends gathered below never fall out." Liked it.*

*"Enough," he cried
and left with all speed
for the neighborhood inn.*

Olive Metcalf

Stagecoach Hill Inn
Sheffield, Massachusetts
01257

Innkeepers: Ann and John Pedretti
Telephone: 413-229-8585
Rooms: 13, all with private bath; one two-bedroom apartment.
Rates: $35 to $50, per room, double occupancy, EP.
Facilities: Open all year. No breakfast, but there are coffee
makers in each room. Lunch May to October, dinner,
bar, lounge. Swimming pool. All major credit cards
accepted.

The inn is located on a winding country road at the foot
of Mount Race. This was a real stagecoach stop all those years
ago.

John and Ann are 🐄 both chefs and, needless to say,
the food is meticulously prepared. There is a very distinct
feeling of England here. Ann is from Lancashire County, and
some of the food reflects this in a most delightful way.
🐄 Steak and kidney pie is here as is steak and mushroom
pie, and, on Saturdays, roast beef and Yorkshire pudding.

The inn also serves a delicious New England oyster pie, and a carpetbagger steak that is stuffed with oysters. At lunch one day I had the thickest Quiche Lorraine I had ever seen, and a salad with a white French house dressing that was delicious. The rolls that came with my meal were fresh, hot, crisp, and yummy.

The dining rooms, done in red and white, are charming. Portraits of the royal family plus a lovely one of Prince Charles and Lady Diana make dining here a very cozy experience.

The pub-lounge with a roaring fire in winter beckons me. The warm, dark paneling, comfortable bar, and a piano complete the picture. English beer on tap is here, of course.

As a special plus for your visit, do see the chalet at the rear of the property. It has hand-stencilled walls and draperies.

There is so much to do in this area it would take a book to tell it all. Come and discover for yourself.

How to get there: Take Exit 2 from the Massachusetts Turnpike. Follow Route 102 west to Stockbridge. Take Route 7 south to Great Barrington and follow Route 41 south to the inn.

⊕

E: *Two chef-owners! How can you miss.*

I love all good inns, but secretly I have a rather special fondness if the boniface is fat.

The Weathervane Inn
South Egremont, Massachusetts
01258

Innkeepers: Anne and Vincent Murphy
Telephone: 413-528-9580
Rooms: Seven, five with private bath.
Rates: $45 to $60, per room, EP.
Facilities: Open all year. Breakfast and lunch served June 15 to end of October. Dinner on weekends. Sunday brunch. Bar and lounge, Robbie Burns Pub in season. Swimming pool, outside games. MasterCard and Visa accepted.

The sign over the bar says, "Kiss the cook." Anne is the chef and pretty enough for a kiss. Chicken soup was bubbling on her stove while I was there, and what an aroma. It tasted even better. Some of Anne's specialties are ☛ Chicken Cordon Bleu, Stuffed Filet of Sole with Shrimp Sauce, and delicious baked ham. I would love to be here for Sunday brunch to try her blueberry pancakes with Canadian bacon.

The dining room is very cheery and bright. Anne

changes the table decor with the seasons.

The inn is so fresh and clean in every corner that you know you have good innkeepers at hand. One of the rooms is named the Norman Rockwell Room because Anne has three of his works on the wall. The first has two youngsters looking at the moon. The second has the youngsters, now a bit older, at the soda fountain, and in the last they are even older, at the registrar's desk getting a license to marry. Anne has some other Rockwell paintings at various places in the inn.

There is one room that needs special mention. It is over the kitchen and has a tiny bathtub with a hand-held shower, really neat.

All the public rooms are comfortable, and the Robbie Burns Pub will keep you totally entertained in season, but there is so much to do in this area year round that you could stay a month.

Bear is the inn dog and is perfect for the part. He is an English cocker spaniel.

How to get there: Follow Route 7 to Route 23 west. You are now 3 miles from South Egremont. The inn will be on your left.

E: *A porch with rockers. Makes an inn.*

Man's cruelty to man knows almost no horizons.
His continued existence, however, is justified
when he says to a stranger, ''Come in.''

Olive Metcalf

The Inn at Stockbridge
Stockbridge, Massachusetts
01262

Innkeepers: Lee and Don Weitz
Telephone: 413-298-3337
Rooms: Seven, five with private bath.
Rates: $40 to $125, double occupancy, EPB.
Facilities: Open all year. Lunch in peak season, dinner by reservation. BYOB. Swimming pool. No credit cards honored, but personal checks accepted.

There is a small red and gold sign by the side of the road directing you into the lane to this lovely inn with stately white columns. Wonderful spot.

Lee's dining room is just beautiful, from the gleaming mahogany table to the sideboards groaning under the weight of her silver services. It is just grand.

The living room-library has soft sofas and chairs, and is done in an intriguing blue print. Plenty of books and a fireplace are at hand. It looks like such a comfortable place to curl up with needlework or a book.

There is a real country kitchen here, spacious and clean.

What a wonderful place to cook.

The rooms are colorful and pleasant. They have king-sized or twin beds and heavy, thirsty, color-coordinated towels that are so important to any inn.

There are 12 acres to roam about in and a large swimming pool to relax in. The trees that surround the whole scene are beautiful.

Lee sometimes can be coaxed to play her piano. This is quite a treat.

How to get there: From the Massachusetts Turnpike, take Exit 2 onto Route 102 to Stockbridge. At the intersection of Routes 102 and 7, take Route 7 north 1.2 miles to the inn's driveway. (Look for the small red and gold sign on your right after you pass under the turnpike.)

E: *The porch is wide and inviting.* *Summer dining is out here, nicely shaded by the trees.*

*"The best landscape in the world
is improved by a good inn in the foreground."*
—Dr. Samuel Johnson

olive Metcalf

The Red Lion Inn
Stockbridge, Massachusetts
01262

Innkeeper: Betsy Holtzinger
Telephone: 413-298-5545
Rooms: 110, 80 with private bath; six suites in summer, two in winter.
Rates: $40 to $80, winter; $40 to $120, summer; double occupancy; EP.
Facilities: Open all year. Breakfast, lunch, dinner, bar. Heated swimming pool. Elevator in summer. Accessible to wheelchairs. Pink Kitty Gift Shop. All major credit cards accepted.

The Red Lion Inn is a four-season inn. In summer you have the Berkshire Music Festival at Tanglewood and the Jacob's Pillow Dance Festival, both world renowned. The inn's own 🐾 heated swimming pool is a nice attraction. Fall's foliage is perhaps the most spectacular in New England; in winter there are snow-covered hills; in spring come the lovely green and flowers. All go together to make this a great spot anytime of year.

The inn is full of lovely old antiques. The halls are lined with antique couches, each one prettier than the next. From a four-poster, canopy bed to beds with great brass headboards, all the rooms are marvelously furnished and comfortable as sin. Whether in the inn itself or in one of the inn's two adjacent places, Stafford House and Ma Bucks, you will love the accommodations. ☞ The wallpaper in Ma Bucks is a delight. All rooms have ☞ extra pillows, which I love.

☞ Excellent food is served in the lovely dining room, or if you prefer, in the Widow Bingham's Tavern. There is an almost-hidden booth designed for lovers in here.

The Lion's Den is downstairs with entertainment nightly, and it has its own small menu. In warm weather the flower-laden courtyard with its Back of the Bank Bar is a delightful place for food and grog.

Blantyre, for those of you who know it, is owned by The Red Lion Inn, and contains 14 of the guest rooms. This is a grand place for an elegant party.

How to get there: Take Exit 2 from the Massachusetts Turnpike and follow Route 102 west to the inn.

♀

E: *Norman Rockwell lived in Stockbridge. The Corner House is a step down the street, so do not miss this great museum of this wonderful artist's works.*

olive Metcalf

Colonel Ebenezer Crafts Inn
Fiske Hill, Sturbridge, Massachusetts
01566

Innkeeper: Pat Bibeau
Telephone: 617-347-3313
Rooms: Six, all with private bath; two suites.
Rates: January 2 to June 30, $55 to $58; $58 to $82, suite.
July 1 to January 1, $60 to $62; $62 to $88, suite. All
rates based on double occupancy, continental breakfast
included.
Facilities: Open all year. Afternoon tea. Publick House nearby
for other meals. Small swimming pool. Near Sturbridge
Village. All major credit cards accepted.

In Colonial times the finest homes were usually found
on the highest points of land. Such a location afforded the
owners commanding views of their farmland and cattle. It
also set them above their contemporaries. So David Fiske,
Esquire, a builder, built this house in 1786 high above Sturbridge. The house has been magnificently restored by the
management of the Publick House, and they have named it
after that inn's founder, Colonel Ebenezer Crafts.

The bedrooms are large, full of good antiques and period reproductions, and offer sweeping views of the surrounding Massachusetts hills.

Patricia Bibeau, the innkeeper, will greet you when you arrive and give you a tour of the house. Do remember to ask to see a bit of the underground railway of Civil War days. The slave hole is still here. These old homes certainly do take you back in time.

Your breakfast of freshly baked muffins, juice, and coffee comes with a copy of the morning paper. Tea and sweets are served in the afternoon, and fruits and cookies are on your night table. To make things just right, you will find your ☞ covers neatly folded back.

When you are ready for some really good food, go two miles down to the famous Publick House in Sturbridge. There you will find some of the best food this side of heaven, including those always-present ☞ sticky buns.

How to get there: Take Exit 3 from I-86, and bear right along the service road into Sturbridge. Continue to Route 131 where you turn right. Turn left at Hall Road and then right on Whittemore Road, which becomes Fiske Hill Road.

E: *Buddy Adler, the innkeeper at Publick House, is justifiably proud of this beautiful old house.*

There is no definition of a proper inn.
Like night and day it either is or is not.

Olive Metcalf

Publick House
Sturbridge, Massachusetts
01566

Innkeeper: Buddy Adler
Telephone: 617-347-3313
Rooms: 21, all with private bath, air conditioning, and phone.
Rates: $47 to $60; suites additional; EP.
Facilities: Open all year. Breakfast, lunch, dinner, bar. Ramp
    to restaurant. TV in lounge. Gift shop. Near Colonel
    Ebenezer Crafts Inn and Sturbridge Village. All major
    credit cards accepted.

Very little has changed at the Publick House in the last
200 years. The green still stretches along in front of it, and the
trees still cast their welcome shade. Not far away, Old Sturbridge Village has been assembled and restored, a living
museum of the past. The Publick House is still taking care of
the wayfarer, feeding him well, providing a bed, and supplying robust drink. Many of the old practices and celebrations
have been revived here. The Boar's Head Procession during
the Christmas holiday is one. They *do* keep Christmas at the
Publick House! All twelve days of it. ☛ Winter weekends

are times for special treats, with chestnuts roasting by an open fire, and sleigh rides through Old Sturbridge Village, a happy step backward in time.

Twenty-one guest rooms have been decorated with period furniture, and the wide floorboards and beamed ceilings have been here since Colonel Ebenezer Crafts founded the inn in 1771. The barn, connected to the main house with a ramp, has been transformed into a restaurant. Double doors, topped by a glorious sunburst window, lead into a restaurant that serves delectable goodies. There is a little musician's gallery, still divided into stalls, that overlooks the main dining room. Beneath this is an attractive taproom, where a pianist holds forth, tinkling out nice noises.

A blueberry patch and a garden which covers more than an acre of land provide the inn with fresh fruit and vegetables during the summer.

I found my way by following my nose around behind the inn to the Bake Shop, where every day fresh banana bread, sticky buns, deep-dish apple pies, corn bread, and muffins come out of the ovens to tempt me from my diet! Take some along for hunger pangs along the road.

How to get there: Take the Massachusetts Turnpike to Exit 9. The Publick House is located on the Common in Sturbridge, on Route 131. From Hartford, take I-84 to I-86, Exit 3, which brings you right into Sturbridge.

E: *The inn's good jams, mustards, relishes, chowders, and more can now be enjoyed at home. They are beautifully packaged and mailed to you wherever you wish.*

Longfellow's Wayside Inn
Sudbury, Massachusetts
01776

Innkeeper: Francis J. Koppeis
Telephone: 617-443-8846
Rooms: Ten, all with private bath, air conditioning, and telephone.
Rates: $30, single; $35, double; EP.
Facilities: Open all year. Closed Christmas Day. Breakfast for house guests only, lunch, dinner, bar. No room service or TV. Pets limited, horses boarded. Gift shop, museum. All major credit cards accepted.

☛ Since 1959 Francis Koppeis has been the innkeeper here, and what a wonderful job he does. Once you meet him you will understand why this famous old inn functions so well and so happily.

Eight generations of travelers have found food and lodging for "man and beast" at the Wayside Inn. Route 20 is the old stagecoach road to Boston, now well off the beaten track. You will find the inn looking much the same as it has for over 270 years, still supplying hearty food and drink, and comfortable beds.

In 1955 the inn was partially destroyed by fire, but the older part was saved. The complete restoration afforded ☞ the chance to put many things back the way they were in the beginning. Many of the nineteenth-century "improvements" were changed. Now part of the inn serves as a museum with priceless antiques displayed in their original settings.

There is a large dining room, and several smaller ones, a bar, a gift shop, and a lovely walled garden. At the end of the garden path is a bust of Henry Wadsworth Longfellow, who was inspired by the inn to link together a group of poems in the fashion of "The Canterbury Tales." "The Landlord's Tale" is known to us all as "Paul Revere's Ride."

Henry Ford bought 5,000 acres surrounding the inn in 1925, and since then this historic spot has been preserved. A little way up the road stand a lovely chapel, the little red schoolhouse that gained fame in "Mary Had a Little Lamb," and a stone gristmill that still grinds grain for the rolls and muffins baked at the inn. I bought some of their cornmeal because ☞ the muffins I ate at the inn were exquisite. This is a most interesting building to visit as all of the equipment in the mill is water-powered.

As a final touch, the inn boasts of the oldest mixed drink in America. It is called ☞ "Coow Woow." You must taste it to discover how well our forefathers lived.

How to get there: From Boston, take the Massachusetts Turnpike to Route 128 north. Take Exit 49 west onto Route 20. Wayside Inn Road is 11 miles west, just off Route 20. From New York, take the Massachusetts Turnpike to Route 495, and go north to Route 20 east. It is approximately 8 miles to Wayside Inn Road.

☙

E: *Only in my country inns do you normally find the innkeeper. And here, when you find Francis, you find a real winner.*

The Wildwood Inn
Ware, Massachusetts
01082

Innkeepers: Margaret and Geoffrey Lobenstine
Telephone: 413-967-7798
Rooms: Five, all share three baths.
Rates: $25 to $45, double occupancy, continental breakfast
   included.
Facilities: Open all year. Breakfast only meal served. For a
   small extra charge there are "country yummies" available. BYOB. Swimming, canoeing. MasterCard and Visa
   accepted.

The Wildwood is a modest, small inn in the town of
Ware. Ware, in turn, is a particularly well-preserved old New
England factory town undergoing a well-modulated renova-
tion.

There is a wraparound porch with rockers which is my
idea of how to while away a summer afternoon. Inside, the
living room is inviting. It is a family room with puzzles,
games, books, an old spinning wheel, an old cradle, and
even ☞ a LIFE magazine from 1937. This was really fun to

page through.

The rooms are each named for the antique quilts on the beds. They are beautiful. For a modern touch, there are dual-controlled electric blankets on each bed.

While they serve breakfast only, they make this meal rather special with very good homemade breads, popovers, peach butter, and much more. The menus of area restaurants are posted for your use. Also, for your drinks they provide ice and pewter goblets.

The Ware River flows by at the back of the inn property, and you will find a canoe for your use to see more of the river. ☞ There is even an old swimming hole at hand. Such fun. The grounds are spacious. There is a hammock in a tree, a grill if you wish to cook, and just lots of room with beautiful trees for idling about.

How to get there: From the Massachusetts Turnpike take Exit 8. Go left on Route 32 about 8 miles until it becomes Ware's Main Street. At second set of working traffic lights, turn left onto Church Street. (South Street is to your right.) The inn is on your right, ¾ mile up where the sidewalk ends.

E: *The hammock in the trees. So restful.*

Cats, birds, flowers and dogs
in companionate confusion are to be found
where hospitality has bested the world of commerce.

Olive Metcalf

The Williamsville Inn
West Stockbridge, Massachusetts
01266

Innkeepers: David and Suzan Saxon
Telephone: 413-274-6580
Rooms: Eight in winter, 14 in summer, all with private bath.
Rates: $58 to $90, double occupancy, EP.
Facilities: Closed three weeks before Thanksgiving and three
    weeks after Easter. Breakfast for house guests only.
    Dinner served Wednesday through Saturday in winter
    and spring, every night but Tuesday in summer and fall.
    Sunday brunch served in winter and spring. Tavern,
    swimming pool, clay tennis court. No pets and no small
    children. Holiday weekend requires a minimum stay of
    three nights. MasterCard and Visa accepted.

The fireplaces in the inn are so nice and so important in
this part of the world where we seem to have so much
winter. Two bedrooms, the dining rooms, the sitting rooms,
and the tavern all have fireplaces. The dining room fireplaces
are raised hearth and especially warming.

Built in 1797 as a farmhouse, the inn is the second

oldest house in the hamlet of Williamsville. The bedrooms are warm and cozy and will welcome you any season of the year. Last time there I slept in a beautiful canopy bed.

There are three dining rooms. The main one is furnished with Windsor chairs. The Library Room is very warm in feeling, and the Blue Room is reserved mainly for breakfast. However, this room does catch the busy summer overflow. In the right weather the screened porch is also used.

The menu is superb, and so is the food. Chicken breast coated with green peppercorn mustard and served with glazed apples is one item. Another offering is scallops in a garlic, shallot, and white wine sauce baked with Gruyère cheese. I had a boneless shell steak coated with black peppercorns and served in a brandy-flavored cream sauce. And not only dinners, but how about for breakfast; fresh fruit, oatmeal, and pancakes with Vermont maple syrup. The fruits are banana, apple, or blueberry.

The bar has a delightful total of two, yes just two, stools, but there are many other spots in the tavern to relax and have your drink.

How to get there: Take the Massachusetts Turnpike to Exit 1 which puts you on Route 41. Turn left toward Great Barrington. The inn is 4 miles south of the turnpike on your right. From the New York Thruway, follow directions for Berkshires Spur, Exit 33. Go south on Route 22 to Route 102, east on Route 102 to Route 41, south on Route 41 toward Great Barrington.

E: *I was lucky enough to be here for a wine tasting when they were searching for additions to their impressive list. We were helped by the two inn cats, Socks and Squeaker.*

Olive Metcalf

The Victorian Inn
Whitinsville, Massachusetts
01588

Innkeeper: Martha Flint
Telephone: 617-234-2500
Rooms: Eight, six with private bath.
Rates: $62 to $82, double occupancy, continental breakfast included.
Facilities: Open all year. Lunch Tuesday through Friday. Dinner every day except Monday. American Express, MasterCard, and Visa accepted.

This wonderful Victorian house, built in 1871, has been treated kindly through the years. One owner (there have been only three) moved in, decided to go to Paris for a vacation, and was so sick on the boat going over that he never came home. Fortunately, he had left a caretaker in his house, so it survived. Several years later when Martha Flint began searching for a country inn to buy, she came here.

☛ Food is the name of the game here. Beautifully served and deliciously different, there are 12 dinner entrees, some purely classic and others wonderfully unique. Desserts are mind-boggling, and there are exotic coffees, too. Our Victorian forebears should have had it so good.

The rooms are delightful, huge, and furnished in a style to match the house. There are three dining rooms, a library, and an elegant drawing room. The hand-tooled leather wainscoting in one room is a marvel, and one of the bedrooms has its original wallpaper. Martha not only has a flair for food, she also is an exceptionally gifted decorator. The picture wall in the little dining room is fair testimony.

How to get there: From the Massachusetts Turnpike take Exit 11 and drive 14 miles south on Route 122 toward Uxbridge. Turn right onto Linwood Avenue where a sign says, "Entering Uxbridge." The inn is 200 yards around that corner, on the right.

E: *The menu cards, circa 1924, bring a charming touch of Art Deco into this lovely inn.*

olive Metcalf

Le Jardin
Williamstown, Massachusetts
01267

Innkeeper: Walter Hayn
Telephone: 413-458-8032
Rooms: Nine, all with private bath.
Rates: Moderate, EP.
Facilities: Open all year. Closed Tuesdays from November 1 to
June 1. Lunch, dinner, Sunday brunch, bar. MasterCard
and Visa accepted.

Hemlock Brook burbles past the sugar maples from
which Walter makes ☛ his own maple syrup. In early
spring each tree is festooned with old-fashioned sap pots,
and in the kitchen there is a huge pot boiling it all down.

The old-fashioned rooms have all been renovated to
make your stay more than comfortable. One of the rooms,
and my favorite, has a canopy bed and a fireplace.

The menu is excellent. There are ☛ four different
salad choices at lunch, and this to me is ideal. Of course there
are sandwiches and hot selections, also. The dinner menu is
more than a little French, though nicely translated into the

112

language of the country. The essence of good food is time, but even the hasty diner is taken care of here with good steaks and chops. The hors d'oeuvres are sinful. The quiche is a Gruyère cheese custard pie. I adore garlic, and the escargots are a garlic lover's dream come true. The entrees are deliciously different, including filet of sole topped with spinach and glazed with a classic, delicate white cream sauce, or chicken with mushrooms in light wine cream sauce inside a pastry shell that is light as a feather. The steak tartare, I learned from a reliable source, is the best ever. Desserts are something else. I can remember sitting at the bar talking with Walter while he plied me with three different calorie-laden desserts he had just made.

The bar is delightful, with comfortable bar stools, tables, an old piano, and most important, a red setter who really runs the inn. His name is Strider.

How to get there: The inn is right on Route 7, just 2 miles south of Williamstown on the right.

E: *Terry Perry is manager of the dining room. She does a superb job.*

Who can refuse the beckoning of a cozy country inn?

olive Metcalf

The Colonial House Inn
Yarmouth Port, Massachusetts
02675

Innkeeper: Malcolm J. Perna
Telephone: 617-362-4348
Rooms: 12, all with private bath.
Rates: In summer, $45, double occupancy, continental break-
fast included; in winter, $35, double occupancy, MAP.
Facilities: Open all year. Lunch, dinner, bar. All major credit
cards accepted.

This was a lovely old sea captain's home, and now is a
lovely old country inn serving some very fine food. At lunch,
the day I was there, the Quiche du Jour was eggplant and the
Crepe du Jour was chicken. I had to have a taste of both and
they were excellent. I also had ☞ lobster salad that was
superb, not all overdressed with dressing, but done just right.
The chef also whips up daily a different cheese dip for your
crackers.

The dinner menu with beautiful treats from the sea,
Tournedos Rossini, steaks, and chicken is a joy. Meals are
beautifully served in one of three intimate dining rooms. The

Oak Room is so named because there are ten different kinds of oak in here. The Colonial Room has hand-stencilled walls, and the Common Room is a glass-enclosed veranda with a view of the garden and a lovely waterfall and fountain.

The rooms are furnished with antiques, comfortable beds, and tons of charm. All have private baths.

This is a very comfortable place to be, shady old oaks and spacious lawns, a rocker on the porch, and good food, plus all the delights of the Cape right at your doorstep. What more can one ask for.

How to get there: Leave Route 6 (the mid-Cape highway) at Exit 7 and go north to Route 6-A. Turn right and in about 1¼ miles, midway between Willow and Union streets, on your right is the inn.

E: *Malcolm, the innkeeper, just makes you feel so at home.*

Well cooked, well served, and well eaten,
a meal at a good country inn.

Olive Metcalf

Old Yarmouth Inn
Yarmouth Port, Massachusetts
02675

Innkeeper: Shane E. Peros
Telephone: 617-362-3191
Rooms: 18, four in inn, two with private bath; 14 in Manor
house next door, all with private bath; air conditioning
and TV.
Rates: $55 to $75, double occupancy, EPB.
Facilities: Inn open all year. Restaurant open April 1 to October 31. Lunch, dinner, and bar. Parking. Near theater
and ocean beach.

The Old Yarmouth Inn is the oldest inn on Cape Cod.
Built in 1696 as a wayside staging inn, it has had many
owners, but it maintains its charm. The building sags a bit,
and when you come in it is like savoring a bit of yesterday,
with old leather suitcases, quaint, papered hat boxes, dusty
coats, hobnail boots, and ancient horse brasses, all combin-
ing to carry you back to the olden days.
There is salt air here, flowers, sunshine, somedays a
little fog. You can dine indoors or out at the Old Yarmouth

Inn, and seafood is, of course, a specialty of the house.

Vegetables, salads, and herbs come fresh from the garden; flaky pastries, rich cakes, and hot breads burst from the ovens.

You are only four miles from the famous Cape Playhouse at Dennis, one of the original "straw hat" theaters. There are several fine beaches nearby, and fishing, boating, and day trips to Nantucket and Martha's Vineyard can be arranged.

How to get there: Leave Route 6 (Mid-Cape Highway) at the Yarmouth Port Exit to Route 6A. Turn right, and one mile will bring you to the Old Yarmouth Inn.

E: *The antique bug is gonna bite me, sure's I live, if I keep coming back to Yarmouth Port.*

*The aroma of freshly baking bread told me surely
I was awakening in a good country inn.*

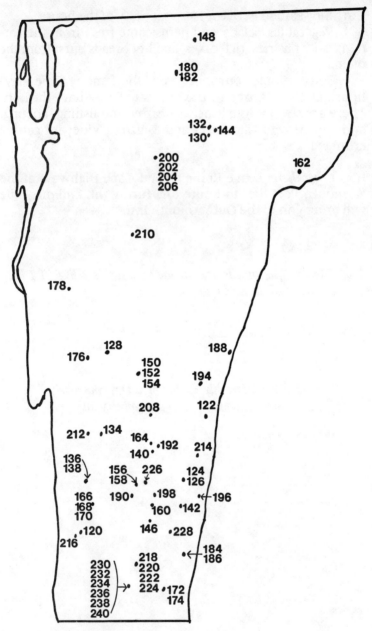

numbers on map refer to page numbers in this book

Vermont

olive Metcalf

West Mountain Inn
Arlington, Vermont
05250

Innkeepers: Mary Ann and Wes Carlson
Telephone: 802-375-6516
Rooms: 12, six with private bath; one apartment with house-
keeping facilities.
Rates: $35 to $48, double occupancy, EP.
Facilities: Open all year. Breakfast, dinner, Sunday brunch,
bar. James Walker Stoneware Studio in the stable-barn.
Hiking, cross-country skiing, fishing, swimming. All
major credit cards accepted.

This inn is truly in the country, with 150 acres of trees,
trails, pastures, and ponds, all on a mountainside overlooking the village of Arlington. Cross the trout-filled Battenkill
River, wind your way over the bridge, which is flower-laden
in summer, go by the millhouse, up past the main cottage
and spring-fed rock quarry, to the seven-gabled inn. ☛ The
grounds around the inn are reputed to have more species of
evergreens than any other place in New England. There are
lovely trails for hiking, jogging, or cross-country skiing, de-

pending on the season.

Wes and Mary Ann are really the ideal innkeepers. From the minute you arrive until you leave you feel at home, warm, and comfortable. Wes loves 🖝 exotic gold fish, and they are in the ponds around the inn in summer and in aquariums in winter. Wes also raises 🖝 African violets. He puts one in each room and invites you to take it home with you. He gave me a speckled beauty for my collection.

The rooms, all named for famous people, are quite different. I was in the Norman Rockwell Room which was up in the treetops. 🖝 A bowl of fresh fruit and a trail map of the property are in each room, a really nice touch. Icelandic comforters and wool blankets are provided to keep you delightfully warm.

They prepare a great Sunday brunch. Eggs Benedict, omelets, and many other tasty dishes are always at hand. I know the eggs are fresh as the farmer came while I was there. His eggs are plump and beautiful.

By the way, Wes has some excellent wines. Wes, Mary Ann, and I had a really good time tasting a nice variety from Wes's cellar.

Old George, the famous old trout, has been caught, but there are a lot of his relatives waiting for you.

How to get there: Midway between Bennington and Manchester, Vermont, exactly a half mile west on Route 313 off historic Route 7, turn onto River Road. Cross the river, and up the hill is West Mountain Inn.

E: *Jim's stoneware studio in the barn displays his work and his wife's. I was fascinated watching him throwing pots on the wheel.*

olive Metcalf

The Inn at Mount Ascutney
Brownsville, Vermont
05037

Innkeepers: Eric and Margaret Rothchild
Telephone: 802-484-7725
Rooms: Nine, five with private bath.
Rates: $38 to $50, double occupancy, continental breakfast
 included.
Facilities: Closed April and November. Dinner Thursday
 through Monday, bar. Skiing nearby. MasterCard and
 Visa accepted.

A country inn that serves ☛ tea at four in the afternoon reminds me of jolly old England. Margaret is a ☛ Cordon Bleu chef, and the inn features country cooking with a
continental flair. The kitchen where Margaret cooks is part of
the dining room, so you watch this fine chef at work.
 The dining room and lounge were converted from an
old carriage house, and they still have the original beams and
an open hearth. There is a small dining room for small
conferences or special parties. A small room overlooking the
meadow is reserved for breakfasts.

The inn is located directly across the valley from the Mount Ascutney ski area. In winter you can sit in the inn and watch the skiers, which is quite a sight at night when the lights are on.

I love inn animals, and here we have a few of them; two cats, Sherlock and Pink, and two Samoyeds, Ebb and Flo.

Whether you're a skier or summer walker, this inn is a great spot for a few days to rub off the trials of everyday life.

How to get there: Take Exit 8 from I-91 northbound, or Exit 9 southbound. Then take Route 5 to Windsor, and proceed west on Route 44. Look for the inn's sign on your right just as you approach Brownsville.

E: *I am a choc-a-holic, and Margaret's own creation is called* *Chocolate Mount Ascutney. Need I say more. Delicious.*

The snow could pile as deep as a mountain
with no worry for me, for I was in the tavern
of a friendly country inn.

Olive Metcalf

Chester Inn
Chester, Vermont
05143

Innkeepers: Tom and Betsy Guido
Telephone: 802-875-2444
Rooms: 31, all with private bath.
Rates: $29, single; $55 to $65, double occupancy; EPB.
Facilities: Closed last three weeks in April and first two weeks
in November. Lunch, dinner every day except Monday,
bar. Heated pool, tennis courts. Skiing nearby. Master-
Card and Visa accepted.

When you arrive in Chester, you will find the Chester
Inn gracing the Village Green. Walk up the steps onto the
large porch with rocking chairs, and on through the door to
the spacious living room with fireplace and great, comfortable furniture. To the left, scout out the real ☛ English pub.
Pass through the door to the pool and patio area outside.
Then pick a favorite spot, and rest a bit.
Some golden October day you might find a covey of
antique cars parked in front of the inn. They don't come
every year, so check with the innkeeper about them if this is

your hobby.

There are seven skiing areas nearby, so for the skier who likes to ski a different area each day of the week, this is the logical place to lodge. After a day on the slopes, return to the inn for a drink in the pub, a gourmet dinner, and then go off to a snug bed. What more could you want? On Saturdays there is even a piano player for entertainment.

The spacious dining room has so much charm, and the heated swimming pool and two, all-weather tennis courts provide plenty of opportunity to exercise after that delicious gourmet dinner.

How to get there: From I-91 take Route 103 to Chester. The inn is on Route 11 on the Green.

E: *There is a shop connected to the inn called ''The Golden Pheasant,'' run by a very charming lady.*

> *The dog nuzzled my leg. The fire sent out a glow.*
> *The drink was good. Only at an inn.*

Cranberry Inn
Chester, Vermont
05143

Innkeepers: Barbara and Michael Yusko
Telephone: 802-875-2525
Rooms: 11, four with private bath.
Rates: From $20 per person, double occupancy, EP.
Facilities: Closed in April. Breakfast and dinner served to house guests. Rooms and restaurant accessible to wheelchairs. Skiing, fishing, and horseback riding nearby. No credit cards accepted.

Traveling down Route 11 one beautiful day I came upon this lovely old inn, a haven for anyone who wants to retreat to the country. Beams abound, and every room was recently redecorated.

There is skiing everywhere around here, and when you come back all cold and rosy from an outdoor day you will be greeted with ☛ a warm fire from a wood burning stove, and pots of steaming, homemade soup. For this I would get cold.

Mike Yusko used to come up here from New Jersey to

ski. Now he and Barbara have come to stay, and are making the Cranberry Inn a must on any list of New England inns.

Your stay here promises to be a memorable one in any month or season. Spring and summer offer fishing, and horseback riding on forest trails, and the wild colors of autumn can be enjoyed from your car, or afoot, or even from your bike. November brings the hunters, and then snow covers every peak and valley. Ski cross-country, or enjoy the slopes at Magic Mountain, Stratton, Bromley, Okemo, Ascutney, Round Top, Killington, or Pico.

How to get there: Turn off I-91 onto Route 103. Follow it to Chester and take Route 11 west to the inn, which is on the right.

🕯🕯🕯

E: *Cranberry glass has long been one of my favorite things. I share my enthusiasm for it with Barbara.*

The good morning greeting and the goodnight good wish can only be found in a country inn.

olive Metcalf

Mountain Top Inn
Chittenden, Vermont
05737

Innkeeper: Bud McLaughlin
Telephone: 802-483-2311
Rooms: 36, all with private bath.
Rates: $80, single; $130 to $160, double occupancy; MAP.
Facilities: Open all year. Breakfast, lunch, dinner, bar, lounge.
Heated pool, lake recreation, tennis, lawn games, pitch
'n putt, game room, horseback riding, sauna, hot tub,
exercise room, cross-country skiing, sleigh rides.
Downhill skiing nearby. American Express, Master-
Card, and Visa accepted.

This is one of the most beautiful inns in New England.
The views are breathtaking. At a 2,000-foot elevation the inn
overlooks Mountain Top Lake, which is surrounded by fantastic mountains.

Everything is here, including crackling fireplaces,
sauna, whirlpool, and the great-and-only 🖝 "Charlie
James" Cocktail Lounge, presided over by a regal fox. There
is a spectacular 🖝 two-story stairway of glass with natural

cherry wood leading down to the lower level, where you will find the dining room and cocktail lounge. Food served here is truly gourmet, with Seafood a l'Indienne, a blend of seafood in a tangy curry sauce with chutney; or braised, boneless chicken breast in honey, rum and pineapple; or crisp duck, lamb chops, and much more. And all so very good.

The rooms, most overlooking the lake and mountains, are large and luxuriously furnished, with king, double or twin beds, and all have spacious baths. A nice touch is your bed turned down at night with a maple sugar candy on your pillow.

Here at the inn they have an excellent ski touring program. To go with it is the old horse barn, where you can relax around antique stoves, sip hot apple cider, and discuss cross-country skiing.

There is ample room for all, with the inn's more than 500 acres. This, with the adjacent National Forest land, gives you 55 miles of scenic trails meandering through mountains that are as beautiful to walk as they are to ski.

The inn has ski-sleds, toboggans, and an ice-skating area, and you alpine skiers are but 20 minutes or less from the Pico and Killington slopes.

How to get there: From Rutland, head north on Route 7. Pass the power station, turn right on Chittenden Road, and follow it into Chittenden. Follow the signs up to the inn.

❦

E: ☛ *Sleighs drawn by ponies or horses are a wonderful yesteryear experience.*

olive Metcalf

The Craftsbury Inn
Craftsbury, Vermont
05826

Innkeepers: John and Susan McCarthy
Telephone: 802-586-2848
Rooms: Ten, three with private bath.
Rates: $45 to $60, double occupancy, EPB.
Facilities: Closed April and November. Dinner, bar. Canoeing,
    swimming, fishing, horseback riding, tennis, and golf
    nearby. MasterCard and Visa accepted.

    The inn is a lovingly restored Greek Revival house that
was built circa 1850. The little town of Craftsbury, said by *The
Boston Globe* to be Vermont's most remarkable hill-town, was
founded in 1788 by Colonel Ebenezer Crafts and lies in what
is called The Northeast Kingdom. The population today is
something less than 700, and that includes Craftsbury, East
Craftsbury, and Craftsbury Common.
    I arrived on a chilly day in the middle of June and was
greeted by a lovely ☛ fire in the TV room. Boy, did it feel
good! Speaking of fireplaces, the one in the living room is the
original fireplace that warmed the first post office in Mont-

pelier, Vermont's capital.

The rooms here are filled with antique wicker, and the double beds have handsome heirloom quilts. Fresh paint and paper have made this lovely old inn even nicer.

 All ice creams, breads, and pastries are prepared here. They also make their own stocks, and this does make a difference in the taste of food.

Country French cooking is how they describe their menu. Cornish game hen with green pepper sauce is but one of the luscious items served. John is the breakfast chef, and he is a whiz at blueberry pancakes or eggs Benedict. The McCarthys raise bees and sell Craftsbury honey, which is a very distinctive honey. They also have their own vegetable garden to ensure freshness.

There is much to do in this area. Rent a canoe, swim in nearby lakes, fish, horseback ride, play tennis, or play golf at Vermont's oldest course in Greensboro where the greens are fenced to prevent intrusion of the grazing cattle. Throughout July and August the Craftsbury Chamber Players perform every Thursday evening. Come and enjoy.

How to get there: Take I-91 to St. Johnsbury, pick up Route 2 west, and at West Danville take Route 15 to Hardwick. Follow Route 14 north to Craftsbury. The inn is on the right, across from the general store.

E: *John hails from Allentown, Pennsylvania where I was raised. Small world.*

Olive Metcalf

The Inn on the Common
Craftsbury Common, Vermont
05827

Innkeepers: Penny and Michael Schmitt
Telephone: 802-586-9619
Rooms: 12, six with private bath, three with fireplace.
Rates: $45 to $70, double occupancy, MAP.
Facilities: Open all year. Food and drinks for house guests
    only. Tennis, swimming, croquet, backgammon. Boat-
    ing and cross-country skiing nearby. Ski touring and ski
    packages.

    If there aren't too many of you, come to The Inn on the
Common. It has grown a little, since Penny and Michael
Schmitt bought the house directly across the street and
added some rooms above ☛ the loveliest craft shop in all
New England. The delectable meals are served in a beautiful
dining room at two lovely, big tables, under the solemn eyes
of two genuine ancestral portraits. Names are provided upon
request.
    Fresh vegetables and herbs come from Penny's own
garden; ☛ her imaginative use of things like sorrel and basil

give meals a definitely different flavor. I hope you'll be here some evening when caviar eggs are on the menu. Your hostess loves to surprise the most sophisticated of diners. You can always get a good piece of beef, fresh brook and rainbow trout caught by local fishermen, and "wild turkey," grain-fed nearby. Six different salad dressings make even the most dedicated salad detester cry for more.

Craftsbury Common is one of the loveliest villages in New England. It was founded in 1789, and many of the buildings date to the late eighteenth and early nineteenth centuries. The gardens in this town are fabulous, including the inn's very own. The Schmitts also have a 150-acre farm in nearby Greensboro, where you can go for nature walks.

The excellent clay tennis court has the most breath-taking view of the Black River Valley and the mountains beyond; a wonderful place for Sam, the inn dog, to live.

How to get there: Follow I-91 to St. Johnsbury, take Route 2 west, and at West Danville take Route 15 to Hardwick. Take Route 14 north to Craftsbury, and continue north into the common. The inn is on the left as you enter the village.

☽

E: The solar-heated swimming pool has a dark painted bottom, flagstone edges, and a little waterfall to let the water in. It disturbs nothing in its peaceful location behind the Common Market.

Olive Metcalf

Shrewsbury Inn
Cuttingsville, Vermont
05738

Innkeepers: Lois and Don Butler, Gil and Kerry Dillon
Telephone: 802-492-3355
Rooms: Three, all with assigned bath; two suites.
Rates: $30 to $40, per person, MAP.
Facilities: Closed mid-April to mid-May, and November. Dinner for non-guests by reservation only; dining room available for private party. Pub lounge. Skiing nearby. MasterCard and Visa accepted.

Lois Butler should have been an interior decorator. She has done such a fantastic job with this marvelous country inn. ☞ All in the family is the theme here. Son, Gil, is the chef. Son, Kerry, is the pub keeper and all-around builder and fixer. Daughter, Pat, is waitress, breakfast chef, bread baker, and creative soft sculpture maker. All under one roof. Wow!

Chef Gil does different things with food. Good examples are ☞ Chicken Livers Marsala and Chicken Breast Dijonnaise. ☞ Scotch Eggs are an unbelievable appetizer.

Outstanding is honest-to-goodness, old-fashioned strawberry shortcake. Remember, this is only a sample of what they have.

Kerry's pub is delightful. In one permanent seat sits Agnes Cornpepper, a lifesize soft sculpture by daughter Pat. No need to ever drink alone here. Agnes is at hand, and so is her new friend, Angus. Wine labels cover the bar and are also on the ceiling above the chandelier. Don takes a real pride in his wine list.

The living room is just as inviting. Lois has done a superb job. One dining room is small and formal, and the other is a grand medieval one with a large table that seats six. Each bedroom is done better than the next. They are all large, airy, and beautiful.

Besides being a wonderful decorator, Lois is also a medieval buff. Everyone in son Gil's wedding was dressed in beautiful medieval costumes, all created right here. The costumes hang about the inn.

This truly is an "inn creeper's" delight.

How to get there: Go north on I-91 to Exit 6, then north on Route 103 to Cuttingsville. You may also go north on Route 7, right on Route 140 in Wallingford, and left on Route 103. The inn is on your left just short of the village.

♥

E: *Mr. Finnegan is the inn cat who looks and acts like one I once had. He has his own ☛ needlepoint sign on the front door telling whether he is in or out. Some class!*

olive Metcalf

Dorset Inn
Dorset, Vermont
05251

Innkeeper: Fred G. Russell
Telephone: 802-867-5500
Rooms: 45, all with private bath.
Rates: $34 to $38, per person, double occupancy, MAP.
Facilities: Closed October to Christmas, and late March to mid-May. Breakfast, lunch, dinner, bar. Parking. TV. Wheelchair accessibility to dining room. Swimming pool. Golf, theater, horseback riding, and skiing nearby. No credit cards accepted.

This is the oldest inn in Vermont, and it has been continuously operated as an inn. There is nothing antique about the welcome you receive, however. The Dorset Field Club, sporting one of Vermont's oldest nine-hole golf courses, extends golf privileges to guests of the inn. ☞ If culture turns you on, the Southern Vermont Arts Center and the Dorset Playhouse will provide the comedy and drama of good theater.

Summer or winter, this is a fine place to stay. In summer, swim in the beautiful pool at the inn, go boating on Emerald Lake, or go horseback riding over old, forgotten roads and past stone fences. There are Wednesday night cookouts that everyone looks forward to.

In winter, there is great skiing within easy driving distance of the inn, and, as in many places, "Ski Weeks" and "Ski Weekends" are featured, with late-arrival snacks, après-ski fondue, hot wine punch, and popcorn.

☛ Bicycle touring is an especially enjoyable enterprise at this lovely inn, with many groups staying the weekends for the fresh air and exercise.

How to get there: Leave I-91 at Brattleboro and go left on Route 30 to Dorset. Or take Route 7 to Manchester Center, and go north on Route 30.

E: *A few years ago, before I ever thought I would be involved in this book, I stayed here on a ski trip. The inn is as lovely now as it was then.*

When you have but one night to spend
which inn to choose is as difficult as
the choice you had years ago at the
penny candy counter, and equally rewarding.

olive Metcalf

Village Auberge
Dorset, Vermont
05251

Innkeepers: Alex and Hanneke Koks
Telephone: 802-867-5715
Rooms: Eight, all with private bath; two suites.
Rates: $50 to $85, EP.
Facilities: Closed April 15 to May 15, and November 15 to December 15. In summer closed Mondays, and in winter closed Mondays and Tuesdays. Breakfast, dinner, bar. Cornucopia Antique Shop. Tennis, golf, swimming, and skiing nearby. MasterCard and Visa accepted.

Stained-glass windows are always lovely, and the one that separates the bar from the dining room is especially well done. Hanneke is an interior decorator and fashion designer by profession. ☞ The inn reflects her talents.

The dining room is just beautiful. It seats only 45 people and is done in shades of warm green. The stunning place plates are a floral pattern from Villeroy and Boch, and Botanica made in Luxembourg. Needless to say, the food served here is extravagant, with hors d'oeuvres and potages such as

Prosciutto and Stewed Prune Relish, Cream of Mustard Soup, and my love, Escargots in Garlic Butter. A special of the day and many more entrees, from veal, steak, sweetbreads, and lamb to fish of the season are always available. Ready for dessert? You must come and taste for yourself and leave your calorie counter in your desk.

The bar is done in rich, warm wood, and is a beauty. There is a fireplace in the lounge. The bedrooms are lovely and the suites are marvelously spacious.

The innkeepers are extremely experienced. Alex attended hotel management school in The Hague, and he has owned and operated restaurants in Haarlem, Holland and Marlboro, Vermont. Hanneke, along with her other talents, operates a unique antique shop right on the inn property.

There is much to do in this area. Three downhill ski areas, cross-country skiing, and the Dorset Playhouse are less than a walk around the block from the inn. Nearby are tennis, golf, and swimming.

How to get there: Take I-91 north to Brattleboro, then take Route 30 to Manchester. At blinking lights take a right and an immediate left, which brings you back on Route 30 north. Go about 5½ miles north of Manchester. Look for the inn on your right.

♔

E: *I have a special fondness for bay windows, and the dining room has a beauty.*

Old Town Farm Lodge
Gassetts, Vermont
05144

Innkeepers: Fred and Jan Baldwin
Telephone: 802-875-2346
Rooms: Ten, two with private bath.
Rates: $35 to $40, per person, double occupancy, MAP.
Facilities: Open all year. Closed on Thanksgiving and Christmas. Breakfast, dinner. BYOB. Parking. Fireplace in common room, game area, horseback riding, cross-country skiing. Downhill skiing, swimming, golf, and fishing nearby. Lodge heated almost entirely by wood. MasterCard and Visa accepted.

If you like to ski and you have youngsters, throw everything in the car and head for the Old Town Farm Lodge. Fred and Jan Baldwin like having kids around, as they brought up their own four children right here. Simple, hearty meals are served with one main course.

The Lodge is located ☛ in the heart of 11 ski areas, both downhill and cross-country, and the Baldwins can direct you to where the skiing is best. They also have their own limited cross-country trails right at the lodge. The Baldwins own two horses, as well as Donovan, the friendly dog. Hunting, fishing, hiking, golf, and swimming are close at hand. The Baldwins have it all, and without the swinging nightlife enjoyed by the singles crowd.

The lodge is busiest during the foliage season, so be sure to reserve ahead if you are going leaf-peeping. The Baldwins are busy all year, restoring and rebuilding the farmhouse that is over 100 years old. It was once known as The Town Farm, because the indigent of the neighborhood were given food and lodging here, in return for a hard day's work. Vermont Maple Syrup is served exclusively, of course.

☞ Cycle Inn Vermont is a bicycle touring service put together by a few Vermont inns, Old Town being one of them. This is a wonderful way to see New England, and also to stay at a different inn each night. Your luggage is transported by car for you.

How to get there: Gassetts is 5 miles north of Chester Depot on Route 10.

E: The handmade spiral staircase that curves to the second floor is beautiful, and it has been painstakingly restored to its original condition.

Were it not for a night's rest in a country inn tomorrow would be but another day.

olive Metcalf

The Old Tavern
Grafton, Vermont
05146

Innkeeper: Lois M. Copping
Telephone: 802-843-2231
Rooms: 35, all with private bath, in five houses.
Rates: $40 to $75, single or double occupancy, EP.
Facilities: Closed in April, and on Christmas Eve and Christmas Day. Breakfast, lunch, dinner, bar. TV in lounge, parking, elevator. Swimming, tennis, nature walks. No credit cards accepted.

Over the hills and far away is a Vermont village called Grafton. The Old Tavern here has been operated as an inn since 1801. Since 1965, when the inn was purchased by the Windham Foundation, it has been restored and is now one of those superb New England inns we all are seeking.

When you turn your car off pounding interstate highways to the tree-shaded route that winds to this quaint village, you step back in time. The loveliest of the old, combined with the comfort of the new, makes this an unbeatable inn. No grinding motors can disturb your slumber when you are in ☞ the best beds in all New England. The sheets and towels are the finest money can buy, and there are extra pillows and blankets in each room. The spacious rooms are filled with antiques, all in mint condition.

There is no "organized activity" at the Old Tavern. ☞ The swimming pool is a natural pond, cool and refreshing. There are tennis courts nearby, and marked trails in the woods for walkers. This is the place to calm your spirits and recharge your batteries.

The cocktail barn is charming, connected to the inn by a covered walk. There are flowers everywhere, hanging in baskets, in flower boxes, and on various tables in the gracious public rooms. The food is excellent, with unusual soups, varied entrees, all cooked well, and served by pleasant waitresses.

☞ Up the street a bit there is a six box stall stable that will accommodate guest horses, plus a four-bay carriage shed, if you care to bring your own carriage. All this for the exclusive use of Old Tavern guests.

How to get there: From I-91 take Exit 5 at Bellows Falls. As you come down the exit ramp, watch for Route 121, which you'll take to the inn.

⚖

E: *The houses across the street that are also part of the inn are enchanting.*

Highland Lodge
Greensboro, Vermont
05841

Innkeepers: Willie and David Smith
Telephone: 802-533-2647
Rooms: 11, all with private bath; 11 cottages.
Rates: $75 to $95, double occupancy, MAP.
Facilities: Closed April 1 to May 25, and after foliage season to
mid-December. Breakfast, lunch, dinner. Beer and
wine license only, setups are available. Parking.
Swimming, boating, tennis. Golf and horseback riding
nearby. MasterCard and Visa accepted.

Highland Lodge is really the place to get away from it
all. With peace and quiet, delicious home-cooked meals, and
the delightful Smith family, you can recharge your batteries
for life easily. But don't mistake me, there is lots to do here in
Greensboro. ☛ Caspian Lake, with the lodge's own beach
house, is just across the road, with swimming, canoeing,
sailing, and fishing. Tennis, golf, and riding are available for
those inclined.

People come back year after year to this friendly place.

There are book-lined walls, puzzles to while away a long afternoon, but mostly, a good mix of genuine, down-home folksiness. It comes over you as soon as you walk through the door. There is a recreation house with supervised play for the youngsters, so a stay here can be a real vacation for parents.

In the fall this is one of the great spots for foliage, and it isn't far to the White Mountains or the Green Mountains. And cross-country skiing in winter is a delight in this un-spoiled country. This area is personally recommended by my publisher, who used to summer in Greensboro. The rooms are decorated beautifully and are very comfortable.

How to get there: Greensboro is 35 miles northeast of Mont-pelier. Take I-91 to St. Johnsbury and follow U.S. 2 west to West Danville. Continue west on Vermont 15, to intersection with Vermont 16 about two miles east of Hardwick. Turn north on 16 to East Hardwick and follow signs west to Greensboro, at the south end of Caspian Lake. Highland Lodge is at the north end of lake on the road to East Craftsbury.

E: *The winter recreation room out back is great for the younger set.*

> *"Drink wine, and live here blitheful while ye may;*
> *The morrow's life too late is, live to-day."*
> — Herrick

olive Metcalf

Three Mountain Inn
Jamaica, Vermont
05343

Innkeepers: Charles and Elaine Murray
Telephone: 802-874-4140
Rooms: Eight, six with private bath; one housekeeping cottage available by the week.
Rates: $40 to $55, per person, MAP.
Facilities: Closed April to June 15, except for special fishing weekends. Breakfast, dinner, pub, lounge. Swimming pool and cross-country skiing. Downhill skiing, tennis, golf, fishing, and horseback riding nearby. No credit cards accepted.

The inn is well named, since it is within a few minutes of Stratton, Bromley, and Magic Mountains. Mount Snow is also within easy range. Skiers should love this location. Cross-country buffs will find a multitude of trails beginning at the inn's doorstep, including a ☛ dramatic trail along the long defunct West River Railroad bed.

This small, authentic country inn was built in the 1780's. The living room has a large, roaring fireplace, complete with an original Dutch oven. The floors and walls are of wide, planked pine, and there are plenty of comfortable chairs. A picture window offers views of the Green Mountains to complete the scene.

A cozy lounge and bar area make you feel very comfortable for sitting back to enjoy good conversation and a before or after dinner drink. ☞ A good wine selection is at hand.

The rooms are tastefully decorated. One room has a four-poster, king-sized bed in it. Another has a private balcony overlooking the swimming pool and garden.

Dinners are a special treat. The menu changes frequently, and you always can be assured of the freshest meats, fish, and vegetables available. Breads, soups, and desserts are all homemade. There are three dining rooms, one with a library, and dinner is always a candlelight affair.

How to get there: Follow I-91 to Brattleboro and take the second exit to Route 30, to Jamaica.

♀♀

E: *There are guided tours for fly fishermen on the West and Battenkill rivers. Write for these package deals, and remember you will eat what you catch.*

If you have never been drawn shivering
from the warmth of a good bed
by the sizzling lure of bacon on the grill,
you have never been in a country inn.

olive Metcalf

Jay Village Inn
Jay, Vermont
05859

Innkeepers: Patricia and Bill Schug
Telephone: 802-988-2643
Rooms: 14, ten with private bath.
Rates: In winter, $42 per person, double occupancy, MAP; in summer, $21 per person, double occupancy, EPB.
Facilities: Closed mid-April to mid-May. Breakfast, dinner, bar. TV in lounge, sports shop, antique shop, trout brook, swimming pool. Cross-country and downhill skiing and golf nearby. All major credit cards accepted.

When you get to Jay you are nearly in Canada, so this makes the Jay Village Inn my most northern Vermont inn. Nestled at the foot of Jay Peak, this is a delightful country inn. Come any time of the year and enjoy the fireplace lounge and bar. It is noted for its après-ski especially, but it's equally pleasurable any season. Sip ☛ a hot buttered rum and enjoy the flaming fire. They have a player piano and some great old songs. Do any of you remember "The Teddy Bear's Picnic"? It is here.

The inn is well known for its American and continental cuisine served in the Galerie d'Art dining room. Pat is the breakfast chef, and her father, Papa Jean, is the dinner chef and well known for his ☛ homemade Parisian bread. I had some, and it was oh, so good. I had ☛ a rack of lamb that was by far the best I have ever eaten. These people are honest to goodness French chefs from France. You will find paintings and objets d'art here inspired by Pat and her French family.

If you are a skier you must know that Jay Peak has one of ☛ the longest, most dependable ski seasons in the east. The aerial tramway is a "trip," and there are exciting trails for every level of skiing, beginner to expert.

For other seasons there are two golf courses in the vicinity, and if you are a hiker you are close to the Long Trail. Summer can be spent by the inn's pool.

And for you antique buffs, they have their own shop right here for your browsing. This is a lovely part of the world.

How to get there: Take I-91 to Exit 26. Take Route 5 north to Route 14 north to Route 100, a total of 8 miles. Go left here for 6 miles to Route 101, then right for 3 miles to Route 242. Go left on Route 242 for one mile to the inn.

E: *An independent spirit and a loveable dog is Barney, the Saint Bernard.*

A night at an inn adds a tinge to the coming day that cannot be described, only enjoyed.

149

Olive Metcalf

The Inn at Longtrail
Killington, Vermont
05751

Innkeepers: Kyran and Rosemary McGrath
Telephone: 802-775-7181
Rooms: 16, 12 with private bath; six suites.
Rates: Vary with season. MAP rates offered fall and winter.
Facilities: Closed April 15 to July 1, and end of foliage season
    to Thanksgiving. Breakfast, lunch in summer only, din-
    ner, bar. Hot tub, music, cross-country skiing, hiking.
    Downhill skiing, swimming, fishing, boating, and sum-
    mer theater nearby. MasterCard and Visa accepted.

Music warms my heart, and here at the inn on weekends during foliage season and sometimes during the week,
you can hear really good ☞ folk and bluegrass music. This
all happens in the pub room, which has a bar 22 feet long and
six inches thick made from a single pine log that was cut just
south of Woodstock, Vermont. They also have a single-seater
bar alongside ☞ the largest boulder I have ever seen inside
a building. It extends 12 feet along the wall and rises right
through the ceiling. The walls are barn wood decorated with

150

antique tools, photographs, and drawings. A wood-burning stove underlines the total comfort of the room.

In the dining room is more of the great boulder, six feet of it. Another wood-burning stove is here. Seating is for 68 people, all of whom can enjoy the large picture windows looking out at spectacular Vermont scenery.

The living room is a large, wood-paneled room with a huge, stone fireplace and comfortable, handmade furniture.

The Appalachian and Long Trails pass alongside the inn, and nearby lakes provide swimming, fishing, and boating. The Festival of Arts at Killington offers folk and jazz concerts. The Green Mountain Guild produces excellent summer theater for your pleasure. As for skiing, you are surrounded by it.

The rooms are small and cozy. The suites are neat, with your own fireplace, color TV, studio couches, and beds, and of course, a full bath.

How to get there: The inn is 8 miles east of Rutland on Route 4 at the Sherburne Pass.

E: *There is a real Irish pub with Guiness on tap and Irish music.*

Hark, which are common noises
and which are the ghosts of long contented guests.

Mountain Meadows Lodge
Killington, Vermont
05751

Innkeepers: Bill and Joanne Stevens
Telephone: 802-775-1010
Rooms: 15, 12 with private bath.
Rates: In winter, $31 to $36, per person, MAP. Lower rates in summer.
Facilities: Closed in May. Breakfast and dinner for house guests. BYOB. TV, game room. Hiking, swimming, boating, fishing. Cross-country and downhill skiing nearby. MasterCard and Visa accepted.

It was here that I met Bear, a mostly red setter, who had just come off the Appalachian Trail carrying his own back-pack. True, I swear. If you are hiking inn-to-inn this is the southernmost inn and a good place to start.

The inn is very casual and relaxed and overlooks 110 acres of lovely Kent Lake. The lake is stocked with 🐟 rainbow trout and largemouth bass. There are boats and canoes for your pleasure. You can swim either in the lake or in the inn's pool.

Vermont home-style cooking at its very best is featured. The inn has a BYOB bar and a game room.

The rooms are fully carpeted and comfortable as sin, but the place to really relax is the large living room which has a big fireplace and lots of windows overlooking the lake. The view is lovely.

The inn has the largest ski touring center in the area, and for you more daring types, Killington and Pico Peak alpine areas are but minutes away.

How to get there: The inn is 10 miles east of Rutland, just off Route 4. Follow Route 4 from Rutland for 12 miles, and at Thundering Brook Road you will come to the inn sign. Turn left. The inn is ¼-mile beyond.

E: Pax and Boots are the inn cats, and Susqua is the gentle inn dog with only three paws.

If all inns were alike they simply would not be inns.

olive Metcalf

The Vermont Inn
Killington, Vermont
05751

Innkeepers: Alan and Judy Carmasin
Telephone: 802-773-9847
Rooms: 14, eight with private bath.
Rates: In summer, $28 to $38, per room, EPB; in winter, $33 to $43, per person, MAP.
Facilities: Closed in May. Restaurant closed Mondays. Dinner, bar. TV, game room, sauna, pool, tennis, lawn games. Gondola ride, summer theater, Norman Rockwell Museum, farmers' market, and skiing nearby. American Express, MasterCard, and Visa accepted.

You may be greeted at the door of this friendly red house by a companionable Labrador named Tammy. Judy and Alan are always here, and a nicer young couple you'll have to travel a long way to find. The Vermont Inn is well-known locally for the fine food served in the lovely dining room. There is also a children's menu, a true help for the traveling family.

Just a sample of the food is tenderloin of pork, so

different, sauteed with fresh mushrooms and flavored in sherry wine with cream. Steak teriyaki is excellent, as is their good selection of fish dishes.

The inn guests are a mixed bag. You'll run into young professional people from Boston or New York, a grandparent or two, families, anyone from honeymooners to golden oldies. Alan has cultivated a fine wine cellar to enhance the good food.

When the Carmasins took over the inn they redecorated all the rooms. Floors were recarpeted or painstakingly restored to the original wood. What a labor of love! This old house has sturdy underpinnings. Some of the original beams still have the bark on them, and how the rocks of the foundation were ever put in place I cannot imagine. Everything was changed around, the old dining room became a lounge to make the inn cosier, so take advantage of the beautiful view of Killington, Pico, and Little Killington, straight ahead across the valley.

Tammy's "Instructions to Guests" on how she is to be treated should be on the *must* list for every inn dog. They are tacked up at the desk. Drop in and read them, then stay awhile.

How to get there: The inn is 6 miles east of Rutland, via Route 4. It is also 4 miles west of the intersection of Route 4 and Route 100 north (Killington Access Road).

🍇

E: *There is a secluded stream, so quiet, just right for meditating, or, if you are brave, to put a foot in.*

The style is the inn itself.

Nordic Inn
Landgrove, Vermont
05148

Innkeepers: Inger Johansson and Filippo Pagano
Telephone: 802-824-6444
Rooms: Three, all with private bath.
Rates: $53.50 to $59.50, per person, MAP.
Facilities: Closed April 15 to Memorial Day. Lunch in winter, dinner, Sunday brunch, bar. Hiking, cross-country skiing. Downhill skiing nearby. American Express, MasterCard, and Visa accepted.

Inger Johansson is the chef-owner of this inn. She is from Kisa, Sweden. While there, she was head chef for the Consul General of Sweden, which makes for Sweden's loss and Vermont's gain. This lady is one of the few 🖙 gourmet chefs in our book. The menu is unusual. The food, whether it is fish, veal, beef, pork, or chicken is different, beautifully served, and a joy to eat. Inger also excels in 🖙 soups and superb desserts.

    The pub lounge downstairs is a nice place to relax, have a cocktail in front of a roaring fire, and reminisce over your day. In winter luncheon is served here. Upstairs, the dining room is a solarium. Imagine the finest food around being served with spectacular views of the winter wonderland forest. With the snow, it is glorious.

The inn is a ski touring center with over 20 kilometers of marked and groomed trails through the Green Mountain National Forest. The inn has complete rentals as well as E.P.S.T.I. instruction. They also offer guided backpack tours from the inn. Alpine skiing is all around the inn.

Filippo and Inger offer their guests a genuine touch of Scandinavia in Vermont. It fits perfectly with the good, New England charm. A nice touch is a fully ☞ licensed masseuse.

The inn cat named Sissy has the most unusual amber-cinnamon eyes I have ever seen on a cat. She shares the inn with a dog, a husky, named Lotta.

How to get there: The inn is between Bromley and Londonderry on Route 11, 14 miles east of Manchester.

♕

E: *Inger made me some of her* ☞ *Swedish pancakes. They looked like a flower on the plate surrounding a great scoop of* ☞ *homemade lingonberry jam and rimmed with fresh whipped cream. Inger took First Prize for her culinary art in the Taste of Vermont.*

> *Having had an excellent meal and*
> *a lovely evening, I tucked myself in bed knowing I*
> *had sinned but it did not seem to matter.*

The Village Inn
Landgrove, Vermont
05148

Innkeepers: Jay and Kathy Snyder
Telephone: 802-824-6673
Rooms: 20, 16 with private bath.
Rates: In winter, $28 to $46, per person, double occupancy,
MAP; in summer, $24 to $45, per room, EPB.
Facilities: Closed April 1 to July 1, and October 20 to mid-
December. Dinner, except on Wednesdays in summer.
Pool, tennis, pitch-and-putt, bumper pool, Ping-Pong,
volleyball, cross-country skiing. Downhill skiing near-
by. All major credit cards accepted.

There is only one question I have about the Village Inn.
Where's the village? This place sits all alone, way out in the
country. Maybe it was the way I came. The Snyders, cordial,
welcoming folks, have a friendly relaxed inn.

The architecture is peculiar to Vermont, with one building built onto another building, onto another. It turns out to
be charming. There are some old rooms, and some new ones,
all spick-and-span and comfortable. The first part of the inn

was built in 1810, and the last additions were made in 1976.

The snows lie heavy around here, and cross-country skiing on miles and miles of marked trails is wonderful. You are only a short hop by car to Bromley, Stratton, Snow Valley, Magic Mountain, or Okemo. Try your luck at ☞ snowshoeing or ice-skating, and after a long day revive yourself in ☞ the whirlpool spa, and then enjoy the fireside warmth in the Rafter Room lounge. There is ☞ a couch in here that needs to be seen!

Summer brings other delights, a neat heated swimming pool, two plexipave tennis courts, hiking through the National Forest, and four-hole pitch-and-putt golf. Summer theater is nearby and riding and hunting are available in season.

How to get there: Via I-91, use Exit 6 at Rockingham. Take Route 103 to Chester, then Route 11 to Londonderry. Continue past the shopping center for approximately a half mile, and turn right on Landgrove Road. Go 4 miles to the Village of Landgrove. Bear left after crossing the bridge and continue one mile to the inn, on your right.

From Manchester, take Route 11 past Bromley Ski Area, and turn left into Peru Village. At the fork in Peru bear left and continue 4 miles through the National Forest to the crossroads in Landgrove. Turn left toward Weston, and the inn wil be on your right.

⧗

E: *Lead me to the bumper pool. I must keep in practice; it's my favorite sport.*

Olive Metcalf

The Highland House
Londonderry, Vermont
05148

Innkeepers: Chris and Tim Hill
Telephone: 802-824-3019
Rooms: Seven, with shared baths.
Rates: $32 to $40, double occupancy, EPB.
Facilities: Closed mid-April to mid-May. Dinner Wednesday
    to Sunday. Beer and wine license. Skiing, hiking, fish-
    ing, and hunting nearby. MasterCard and Visa accepted.

The Highland House dates back to 1840, and the wide
pine floorboards are good proof of its age. The rooms are
comfortable and neat. And the innkeepers are young and
energetic. Here is another inn that will improve a bit each
year because of its fine innkeepers.

There is a wood stove in the dining room, and lovely
plants are in abundance. Fresh food is the order of the chef.
All ☛ the sauces, salad dressings, breads, and desserts are
made right here under his watchful eye. Roast New England
duckling, a favorite of mine, is slow-roasted until crisp, and
then is served with the chef's sauce du jour. To give you just

160

another touch of his cooking, Veal Milanaise is served with Spaghetti Marinara. ☛ This is fine food served in a lovely small dining room.

Magic Mountain and Stratton Mountain are nearby ski areas. The Green Mountain National Forest is close at hand for hiking, fishing, hunting, or cross-country skiing in season.

This is a wonderful part of New England right on famed Route 100 which runs up the spine of Vermont. Plenty of antique shops and other shops to keep you busy.

How to get there: Take Exit 2 from I-91 at Brattleboro. Take Route 30 north to Route 100, and the inn is just north of town on Route 100.

E: *The inn sits back from this fine old road in the midst of a lovely, expansive lawn.*

Insomnia is almost a blessing if you are in an inn within easy earshot of a country church bell.

Olive Metcalf

Rabbit Hill Inn
Lower Waterford, Vermont
05848

Innkeepers: Eric and Beryl Charlton
Telephone: 802-748-5168
Rooms: 20, all with private bath.
Rates: $31 to $57, double occupancy, EP.
Facilities: Closed four weeks in early spring and after foliage
season to mid-December. Breakfast, dinner, bar. Cross-
country skiing. MasterCard and Visa accepted.

There is a sign in the dining room in Gaelic. It means
100,000 welcomes, and these warm, friendly innkeepers
mean just that.

The dining room has wide floorboards, a Franklin-type
wood stove, and pewter and brass from the Charlton's own
collection. It is bright, airy, and the setting for fine food. The
innkeepers' selection is a nightly dinner special chosen from
the best the kitchen can conjure up, which is always a good
choice. There are, of course, many other entrees including
steak, lamb, veal, fish, and chicken. Do try ☛ Breast of
Chicken Devonshire served with a sauce of tangy orange,

honey, and vermouth. Delicious!

Bedrooms are large and comfortable. Some have fire-places, canopy beds, love seats, and all face east with a view of the Presidential Range. The porch on the second floor is a special spot for me to just sit, rock, and look.

There also is a library on the second floor full of good books. Please, when you take a book from this inn, or indeed any inn, send it back when you are finished.

The Briar Patch is the ski shop. It has instructions and rentals. The trails are beautiful, winter or summer, winding along and across Mad Brook with its beautiful waterfalls, then on across pastures and deep into lush, wooded areas.

There is a lot of history up here, and this lovely village is on the most photographed list in Vermont.

How to get there: Take Route 2 east from St. Johnsbury and turn right onto Route 18. Or coming from Route 5, take Route 135 east to Lower Waterford.

E: *Many interesting musicians live nearby, and they wander into the inn to entertain. How nice.*

"Venite ad me ownes qui stomacho laboratoratis
et ego restaurabus vos."
"Come to me all whose stomachs cry out in anguish
and I shall restore you."

The Okemo Inn
Ludlow, Vermont
05149

Innkeepers: Rhinard and Toni Parry
Telephone: 802-228-2031
Rooms: 12, ten with private bath, some with brass beds.
Rates: $45 per person, double occupancy, MAP. Five-day ski and golf packages available.
Facilities: Open all year. Breakfast, dinner, liquor license. Fireplaces in public rooms. Swimming pool, sauna, cross-country ski trails. Downhill skiing and golf nearby.

Two little brown dogs named Fred and Barney welcome you when you arrive at Okemo Inn. Fast on their heels come the Rhinard Parrys, a hard-working young couple. Their house has been here since 1810, but there's nothing old-fashioned about the swimming pool. And ☛ the spacious sauna is the very thing to take the ache away from the first day of skiing.

Meals are served family-style, and are hearty, home-cooked, featuring roast beef, ham, turkey, chicken, and if that fare seems a little plain, how about a little Stroganoff

164

just for variety?

The inn is practically at the foot of Okemo Mountain, a fast-growing, popular place to ski. Both downhill and cross-country skiing are enjoyable in this area. This seems an ideal spot for a couple, or young family, who love skiing.

The inn has a liquor license, and there is a working fireplace and color TV in the lounge.

A collection of "necessary china" for bedroom use in times bygone is displayed on the bookshelf in the second floor hall. It's a wonder.

How to get there: Take Exit 6 north from I-91, and follow Route 103 to Ludlow. The inn is located one mile from Okemo Mountain public transportation, which includes Vermont Transit buses and Amtrak trains to Bellows Falls, and 25 miles from Springfield or Rutland Airports.

E: *The Parrys have an 1896 Edison gramophone that works.*

A night at an inn adds a tinge to the coming day
that cannot be described, only enjoyed.

Olive Metcalf

The Inn at Manchester
Manchester, Vermont
05254

Innkeepers: Harriet and Stan Rosenberg
Telephone: 802-362-1793
Rooms: 14, seven with private bath.
Rates: MAP rates in winter, EPB rates in summer, furnished upon request.
Facilities: Closed in April and November. Breakfast, dinner, beer and wine license. TV, Ping-Pong, fireplaces in public rooms. Swimming pool. Skiing, golf, tennis, and theater nearby. American Express accepted.

When you walk in the door of the inn you may be greeted by the inn dog, a Saint Bernard named Christy. In any case your eyes will light on the beautiful greenery in the bay window of the living room. The inn has been well restored and is full of good antiques. The many fireplaces with comfortable sitting areas surrounding them, and a dining room that has ☛ Tiffany lamps, add up to a warm country inn.

The accommodations are of two types. A bunk room

and singles are on the third floor, all with carpets and great views.

The rooms a floor below, are extremely clean, all with good, new beds, and some with antiques. They are done in bright colors, yellows and blues, with dust ruffles that are color-coordinated. All are very nice.

The food is homemade, even the breads, and is served family-style. Apple pancakes with local maple syrup can start anyone's day right. When my publisher heard that one of the desserts was apple crisp with ice cream, I had to tie him to his chair.

The inn is conveniently located in the heart of just about everything, with skiing, downhill and cross-country, only minutes away. Summer brings great antiquing, summer theater, specialty craft shops, and boutiques. Golf and tennis are within walking distance of the front door. This really is a lovely area.

The game room has TV, Ping-Pong, card tables, and a warm fireplace. Very nice.

The barn is being utilized by groups of artists under the direction of Charles B. Hayward. Any interested artist may contact the inn for dates and rates.

How to get there: The inn is approximately 22 miles north of Bennington, Vermont on Route 7. It is on the left.

E: *The shoulder of Equinox Mountain is out the back door and in autumn is a sight to behold.*

Olive Metcalf

The Reluctant Panther
Manchester Village, Vermont
05254

Innkeepers: Edward and Loretta Friihauf
Telephone: 802-362-2568
Rooms: Seven, all with private bath, TV, and phone, four
    with fireplace.
Rates: $45 to $65, double occupancy, EP.
Facilities: Closed November 1 to mid-December, and mid-
    April to Memorial Day. Breakfast, dinner, bar, lounge.
    Elevator. No pets. No children. Golf, tennis, hiking, and
    skiing nearby. American Express, MasterCard, and Visa
    accepted.

The inn is mauve on the outside. A color I love, and a
color you cannot miss. This is a very special inn in many
ways. As an example, there is a greenhouse for dining which
makes a perfect atmosphere for the fine food served here. I
love it when I find something different on a menu like
🖝 hickory-smoked Canadian bacon rolled around stalks of
asparagus and covered with a hot, tasty cheddar cheese
sauce; and this is only a first-course dish. On the entree list is

breast of chicken stuffed with almonds and tart apples. The way they serve trout or any of the other entrees is an art in itself. Must be fun to work in this creative kitchen.

The rooms are unique. The rugs go right up the walls and where they do not there are mad wallpapers. Every room is an experience unto itself. Four of the rooms have ☞ fireplaces that work.

A very nice touch is ☞ a tiny elevator for those of you who have problems with stairs.

Golf and tennis are nearby, also all kinds of walking and hiking, and, of course, shopping, one of my favorite pastimes. And in winter you have downhill and cross-country skiing at every turn.

How to get there: As you approach Manchester from the south on Route 7 keep an eye on the left and soon the *mauve* Reluctant Panther will pop into view.

E: *In the bar over in a corner is a stuffed bear. I like him.*

The Worthy Inn
Manchester Village, Vermont
05254

Innkeeper: Barbi Mouat
Telephone: 802-362-1792
Rooms: 25, all with private bath.
Rates: $30 to $36, double occupancy, EP. Special package
    rates available.
Facilities: Open all year. Breakfast, lunch in July and August,
    dinner. Bar, lounge, pool, tennis. Golf and skiing near-
    by. American Express, MasterCard, and Visa accepted.

Many moons ago when I was still skiing we would stay
here at this inn. In those days we called it the Worthless Inn,
but you surely could use that name no more. Things have
changed, and Barbi has a very nice inn. Built in 1889, it has
some delightful Victorian touches.

The upstairs halls were being ☛ hand-stencilled while
I was there. Rather nice to see. The rooms are all slowly being
done over in antiques and ruffled curtains. This inn is going
to become better and better.

There is a large fieldstone fireplace in the living room

with comfortable couches and chairs around it. The taproom is neat with a lovely bar and tables and chairs. Nice any time of-the year.

Food served here is excellent. The breakfasts are really ☛ hearty; eggs in any style including Benedict, blueberry or plain pancakes, muffins, and more and more. The dinners are also expansive, ☛ veal served six different ways, beef five ways, topped by the chef's Drunken Chicken, a real winner. Here is a chef who is not only very, very good, but also is one who thoroughly enjoys his work.

The swimming pool and patio area are very pretty, surrounded by well-trimmed lawns and old birch trees. This would be a good spot for a summer wedding.

There is so much to do in this area, golf, skiing, alpine slides, Equinox Skyline Drive, antique shops, and just walking and enjoying.

How to get there: Coming north on historic Route 7A you will find the inn on your left right in Manchester Village.

E: *The rockers on the front porch make it summer for me.*

The Four in Hand
Marlboro, Vermont
05344

Innkeepers: Peter and Sheila Kane
Telephone: 802-254-2894
Rooms: Six, all with private bath.
Rates: $40, double occupancy, continental breakfast included.
Facilities: Open all year. Lunch in season, dinner, pub. Entertainment. Near skiing. MasterCard and Visa accepted.

It is so nice when an inn that was in an earlier edition of the book makes a comeback. These energetic people have really made over this inn and done a wonderful job.

The rooms, all doubles, are fresh and comfortable. The owners also have developed a delightful common room where you can have coffee, read a paper, or just chat.

Richard Caplin is now the chef and a good one. He was the sous-chef before, so he has good background for his job. He plans no changes in this inn's excellent menu. I feel sure when you sample one of Richard's Four in Hand dinners you will agree that he is a lucky find for inn lovers. Try his special. It is always good.

The food is country French, and this young man really knows what it is all about. The desserts are sinful, and the wine cellar is a beauty.

 The Backdoor Pub is a treat, great for relaxing after skiing in front of a roaring fire. All is here from a good hot toddy or just about anything else you wish to drink, to burgers, chili, and hot dogs. Local entertainment is on Fridays, and during the school year there are films on Thursday evenings.

This is a nice family venture.

How to get there: From I-91 take Exit 2 at Brattleboro, then Route 9 west to Marlboro. The inn is on the right.

E: *The cat is named Jiggs, an orange cat. Orange cats are always good inn cats.*

Olive Metcalf

Longwood Inn
Marlboro, Vermont
05344

Innkeepers: Tom and Janet Durkin
Telephone: 802-257-1545
Rooms: 13, 11 with private bath.
Rates: $55 to $85, double occupancy, EPB.
Facilities: Open all year. Closed Christmas Eve and Christmas
Day. Breakfast, lunch during music festival and foliage
season, Sunday brunch. Dinner daily in season and
Thursday through Sunday out of season. Bar. Music
and skiing nearby. MasterCard and Visa accepted.

The copper lanterns at the door of this over 200-year-
old inn are worth a visit in themselves. The inn has worn
many faces through the years. It was first a dairy farm
known as the Five Maples, when milk was eight cents a
quart, then a halfway house, a college dormitory, a local
theater, and now an engaging country inn.

Any time of year is a good time to come to the Longwood Inn. In the summer, in nearby Marlboro, the
☛ world-renowned music festival takes place, and in the

174

fall, there's the Bach Music Festival. In winter, ski downhill or cross-country at nearby areas, or when the roads are clear, bring your bicycle or rent a horse and see this marvelous area in a more leisurely fashion.

The most important ingredient found at Longwood's restaurant is the restful luxury of dining in leisure. The menu invites you to partake of homemade soups, fresh vegetables, a Caesar salad prepared at your table, fish, beef, or chicken. Veal and pasta dishes are specialties of the house. Ask for ☞ the special mulled cider or grog in fall and winter. All are creatively prepared. Desserts are delectable. All bread and desserts are made daily in their kitchen. Breakfasts are delicious, and include fluffy pancakes and French toast with local pure Vermont maple syrup. Oh my, what a way to go.

How to get there: From I-91 take Exit 2 at Brattleboro. Take Route 9 west to Marlboro. The inn is on the right.

♫

E: *Barnaby, the inn cat, really runs the inn with an iron paw.*

> *The groaning breakfast board*
> *of a good inn always makes it difficult*
> *to remember the word ''diet.''*

Olive Metcalf

Red Clover Inn
Mendon, Vermont
05071

Innkeepers: Dennis and Bonnie Tallagnon
Telephone: 802-775-2290
Rooms: 15, eight with private bath.
Rates: $35 to $45, per person, double occupancy, MAP.
Facilities: Closed mid-October to Thanksgiving, and mid-April to mid-June. Breakfast, dinner, bar. TV, swimming pool. Skiing nearby. All major credit cards accepted.

In the center of Vermont, just five miles east of Rutland, is a flower of a country inn. (Wish I had said that but, in truth, it is on their brochure.) The red clover is the state flower of Vermont. The inn is the former summer home of General John Woodward.

This is a very comfortable inn. The living room has cozy couches and chairs, and the tavern is a delightful spot to unwind in. Curl up in front of the fire with a good book and let the world whirl on by itself.

Owner-chef Dennis was ☞ tutored by his father and

apprenticed in his kitchen in Switzerland. He is a fine chef. Dinner is served by candlelight. Fresh vegetables and fruit from their own garden and local farms are served here.

Breakfast is not just a ho-hum thing. It is for real, with home-baked breads and muffins, omelets, and pancakes.

☛ The view from the pool is beautiful. This is great country for hiking, biking, cross-country and downhill skiing, snowmobiling, or just resting.

How to get there: Take Route 4 east from Rutland, and the inn is on the right, down narrow Woodward Road.

E: *Sundance is an inn horse. His friend is Four Square, recently retired from Skidmore College.*

*Even the riches of Kubla Khan cannot sway
the evenhanded hospitality of a proper innkeeper.*

Middlebury Inn
Middlebury, Vermont
05753

Innkeepers: Frank and Jane Emanuel
Telephone: 802-388-4961
Rooms: 79, 61 with private bath and air conditioning.
Rates: $34, single; $44 to $66, double; EP.
Facilities: Open all year. Breakfast, lunch, dinner, bar. Parking. Elevator, TV, gift shop. Skiing and bicycling nearby. All major credit cards accepted.

There has been an inn standing at this same location since 1788. There have been some changes, due to fire and the inroads of time, but the present brick building was constructed in 1827. One hundred years later, when the Middlebury Hotel Company took over, a new heating plant was installed, and extensive repairs were made. The inn has a good central location, and, of course, anyone who has anything to do with Middlebury College knows about the inn.

It is being managed now by Frank and Jane Emanuel and was recently awarded a restoration project grant by Vermont's Historic Preservation Division. There is a delightful veranda café, and a really large lobby. ☞ The dining room is beautiful, and the food that is served here is delicious. Upstairs the wide halls wander and dip, up one step and down three, wide enough for those ladies of long ago to have maneuvered their hoopskirts with grace.

How to get there: Go up Route 7, and you run right into Middlebury. The inn is in the middle of town.

E: *I could stay forever, mooning over the jigsaw puzzles in the lobby or eating their nightly popovers.*

Our sympathy for the hardships of our forbears should be somewhat mitigated by the fact that they had the best of country inns.

Olive Metcalf

Zack's on the Rocks
Montgomery Center, Vermont
05471

Innkeepers: "Zack" and Gussie Zachadnyk
Telephone: 802-326-4500
Rooms: One cottage, sleeps two.
Rates: $60 per night, EP.
Facilities: Open all year. Closed Mondays and Christmas Day.
Dinner by reservations only, bar. MasterCard and Visa
accepted.

After you finally find Zack's you really will not believe
what you see. His cottage home, and restaurant are literally
hanging on the rocks over an incredible valley.

This is my smallest inn. A cottage that sleeps two has a
living room, dining ell, kitchen, two fireplaces, a bedroom,
and a *wow* of a bathroom with a sunken tub. Even if you
cannot stay here, stay in town and come up here to eat Zack's
food. It is ☞ fantastic, and so are he and Gussie, his wife.

How to explain Zack's is almost impossible. When you
approach the door of his restaurant you will find it is locked.
Ring the sleigh bells, and the door will be opened by Zack. He

will be in a wondrous costume and the ☞ performance begins. I will tell you no more except about the food. The menu is printed on a brown paper bag which is in beautiful contrast to his restaurant and Gussie's bar. Zack does all of the cooking. He is the most ☞ inventive chef and innkeeper I have had the pleasure to meet. The dining room has to be seen to be believed.

And Gussie's bar is something special. It has an organ with a full grand piano top built over it. This is my first ☞ organ bar. The room has a stone fireplace and is done pub style but with a flair. The bar has but five stools, but to go with it is the best stocked back-bar in Vermont. To top it all the inn plays music from the '40s. What a pleasant sound.

The inn dog is Gypsy, the largest German shepherd north of the Mason-Dixon line, and probably below as well. Pyewacket is a noisy Siamese cat who runs the inn and Zack.

Reservations here are an absolute must.

How to get there: Going north from Stowe on Route 100, turn left on Route 118 at Eden. When you reach Montgomery Center, turn right on Route 58. The inn is up the hill on the left, after the road becomes dirt.

⚖

E: *Zack's cottage is called Fore-the-Rocks. The private home is called Off-the-Rocks, and the inn is called On-the-Rocks. Gussie's bar is After-the-Rocks. Lots of rocks up here.*

olive Metcalf

Black Lantern Inn
Montgomery Village, Vermont
05470

Innkeepers: Rita and Allan Kalsmith
Telephone: 802-326-4507
Rooms: 11, ten with private bath.
Rates: In winter, $35 to $40, per person, MAP; in summer,
$35 to $40, double occupancy, EP.
Facilities: Closed first two weeks in May. Breakfast, dinner,
bar. Parking. TV in lounge, fireplace in sitting room.
Cross-country skiing. Downhill skiing, fishing, swim-
ming, golf, and tennis nearby. MasterCard and Visa
accepted.

When you get to Montgomery Village you are nearly in
Canada, perhaps six or seven miles from the border. This is a
quiet Vermont village, and the Black Lantern has been nicely
restored by its hard-working owners. Whether you come in
the snow for a skiing vacation, or on a green summer day,
there is a warm welcome at this friendly inn. It is also
surprising to encounter a rather sophisticated menu in this
out-of-the-way corner of the world.

You can ski at Jay Peak, where there are 50 miles of trails for every kind of skier, outright novice to expert. Not too far away, over the border, there are four Canadian mountains, and ski-week tickets are available. Cross-country skiing starts at the inn door, and is undoubtedly the best way to see beautiful Vermont in the winter.

Summer brings the joy of outdoor life. Fishing, swimming, golf, tennis, and hiking are all very near. You've heard about those country auctions, haven't you? Or would you rather spend the day browsing through antique shops? Whatever you choose to do, there will be a superbly quiet night to catch up on your sleep.

The double-peaked roof on this nice, old, 1803 farmhouse covers a typical north-country inn. Small, friendly, and just a little bit different.

How to get there: Go north from Stowe on Route 100, and turn left on route 118 at Eden. This will take you into Montgomery Center. Continue down the main street and out of town, and before too long you will reach Montgomery Village and the inn. From I-89 in Burlington, turn right at St. Albans onto Route 105, toward Enosburg Falls. Pick up Route 118 at East Berkshire, and follow it to Montgomery Village and the inn.

🐓

E: *What is there that is so special about yellow cats? The youngster that greets you at the door is a charming feline.*

olive Metcalf

The Four Columns Inn
Newfane, Vermont
05345

Innkeepers: Jacques and Sandy Allembert
Telephone: 802-365-7713
Rooms: 12, all with private bath, most with air conditioning.
Rates: $50 to $75, double occupancy, continental breakfast
    included. Special ski packages available.
Facilities: Closed April, November, and on Tuesdays from
    May to October. Lunch July through October; dinner,
    jacket required. Bar, TV. Parking. Swimming, hiking,
    skating. Skiing nearby. MasterCard and Visa accepted.

If the hearty goodness of your New England cooking
should be starting to pall, turn your wheels toward The Four
Columns Inn in Newfane. Here in an authentic New England
village, in a lovely old house, you will find 🖙 superb continental cuisine with a menu that will tease every palate.

🖙 Trout "au Bleu," plucked living from the inn's own
tank, Curry Indonesian-style, assorted hors d'oeuvres Pari-
sienne, fresh Salmon Bernaise, rack of lamb for two, and
many other delectable dishes are served.

Jacques Allembert came to The Four Columns from Le Bistro in New York City several years ago. He inherited the complete, fine staff of the inn from the previous innkeepers.

Many of the rooms were made from the old barn that is connected, Vermont-style, to the house. Though the beams are rough, the freshness of the decor belies the house's age.

☛ The wine list is excellent, as is to be expected, and it is also possible to obtain good American wine by the glass.

In winter skating is fun on the inn's trout pond. Skiing, either Alpine or cross-country, is nearby. Summertime swimming in their pool, hiking, or just sitting under a willow tree and dreaming are sheer delight.

How to get there: The inn is 220 miles from New York, 100 miles from Boston. Take Exit 2 from I-91 at Brattleboro to Route 30 north. The inn is in Newfane, 100 yards off Route 30 on your left.

E: *Sitting in front of the fireplace, candlelight, soft music, and oh, the food. It is all so perfect.*

*I often wonder if a war could start
if the heads of confronting nations spent an evening
at a proper tavern.*

olive Metcalf

Old Newfane Inn
Newfane, Vermont
05345

Innkeepers: Eric and Gundy Weindl
Telephone: 802-365-4427
Rooms: Ten, eight with private bath.
Rates: $65 to $85, double occupancy, continental breakfast included.
Facilities: Closed April to mid-May, late October to mid-December, and on Mondays. Lunch in summer and fall, dinner, bar. Parking. Skiing nearby. No pets. No credit cards accepted.

The inn is well named, for old it is, 1787 to be exact. It has been carefully kept, however, and the weary traveler will find great comfort and fabulous food.

Almost all the rooms have twin beds. The rooms are large and tastefully furnished. Gundy has beautiful taste in her decorating. There is an informal bar and lounge, and the dining room has tables with pink cloths over white ones. Very effective. There is a huge brick wall with fireplace in the dining room that gives a wonderful feeling of warmth and good cheer. The floors here are polished to a turn and beyond. And not just run-of-the-mill glassware for the inn. The drinks I had before lunch were served in crystal.

Eric is a fine chef. His soups are a bit different and very good. I have tried both the cold strawberry and creamed watercress. Loved them both. By the way, I hate calves liver, but Eric asked me to try his. What magic he performed I do not know, but I ate every bite. Veal is king here. Eric butchers his own, so he gets the exact cuts he wants. Of course the menu also has seafood, lamb, fowl, and fine steaks. The dessert menu reads like poetry from the flaming suzette and jubilee to a fabulous omelette surprise. There are also some cream pies that demand that you do not even think of calories.

How to get there: Take Exit 2 from I-91 in Brattleboro, and follow Route 30 north. The inn is on Route 30, on the left in Newfane.

✸

E: Gundy arranges pillows on the beds just beautifully.

> Come away, O human child!
> To the waters and the wild
> With a faery hand in hand . . .
> —William Butler Yeats

Olive Metcalf

The Inn at Norwich
Norwich, Vermont
05055

Innkeepers: Alden and Doreen Twachtman
Telephone: 802-649-1143
Rooms: 21, 19 with private bath; two suites with kitchen facilities; TV in all rooms.
Rates: $45 to $70, double occupancy; $70 to $90, suites; EP.
Facilities: Open all year. Breakfast, lunch, dinner, bar. Swimming, canoeing, golf, and skiing nearby. MasterCard and Visa accepted.

Right on the sign for the inn it says, "Since 1797," and it is truly said, because travelers up the beautiful Connecticut River Valley have been finding a warm welcome at this grand old house ever since. Just a mile away from Dartmouth College, alumni, skiers, tourists, and commercial travelers find here a special homelike atmosphere that is dignified but fun. A treat at hand for music lovers is the ☛ Hopkins Center in Hanover.

You can come to Norwich by air, car, bus, or rail, or walk if you must, but do come. Reserve well ahead during football weekends, for this is the place to be. There is a great room downstairs in the inn where the thick stone foundation of this old building is revealed, and it is here the losers and winners drown or celebrate their fortunes.

The food is very good, really exceptional. Rack of Lamb or ☞ Norwich Inn Scallops are a treat, as is the Duck à l'Orange. The salad bar is one of the best I have found. Good also are the homemade breads. Lunch has a wide, good menu, but my favorites are the soup and salad combinations.

The big bow window in the dining room is a delight, but I think I like best to eat on the beautiful ☞ flower-filled porch, which is even used in the winter. You must see it in the snow.

With Hanover and Dartmouth right at hand you can find one good thing after another to do in all seasons in this lovely area of Vermont and New Hampshire.

How to get there: Take Exit 13 from Route I-91. Go west a bit less than a mile to the center of town. The inn is on your left.

🔔

E: *A perfect drink spot is the dear little Victorian bar off the living room.*

Choose your inn, and enter in the world of relaxation.

olive Metcalf

Johnny Seesaw's
Peru, Vermont
05152

Innkeepers: Gary and Nancy Okun
Telephone: 802-824-5533
Rooms: 22, all with private bath; ski bunk rooms.
Rates: In summer, $13 to $26, per person, EPB; in winter, $30 to $55, per person, MAP.
Facilities: Closed end of skiing to July 1, and end of foliage until Thanksgiving. Breakfast, dinner, liquor license. Parking. TV, game room, swimming, tennis. Skiing, hunting, golf, horseback riding, and fishing nearby. MasterCard and Visa accepted.

The food at the inn is good, tasty country food prepared with imagination, featuring home-baked bread and home-made soup. Val is the fine lady chef who turns out all this fine fare.

The inn has a unique character, mostly because of the guests who keep coming back. It is set 2,000 feet up, on Bromley Mountain. The 65 by 25-foot pool, marble-rimmed, is a great summer gathering place, and the tennis court is always ready. There are six nearby golf courses, and riding is offered at the Ox Bow Ranch near Weston.

For the many skiers who come to Vermont, Bromley's five chairlifts and GLM Ski School are right next door. Stratton and Magic Mountains, the Viking Ski Touring Center, and Wild Wings X-C, are but a few minutes away.

For fishermen and hunters, or those who wish to take up the sport, the Orvis Fly-Fishing and Wing Shooting Schools in nearby Manchester have classes. The sportsman classes are held twice weekly, in three-day sessions through October, and participants may stay at the inn. The nearby towns boast many attractive and interesting shops.

How to get there: The inn is 220 miles from New York, 150 from Boston. From Route 7 take Route 30 right at Manchester Depot. The inn is 10 miles east, on Vermont Route 11. From I-91, follow Exit 6 to Route 103 to Chester. The inn is 20 miles west, on Vermont Route 11.

E: *The circular fireplace in the lounge really attracts me, to say nothing of the cushioned platform along one side of the room.*

*Cats, birds, flowers, and dogs
in companionate confusion are to be found
where hospitality has bested the world of commerce.*

Olive Metcalf

Okemo Lantern Lodge
Proctorsville, Vermont
05153

Innkeepers: The Racicot Family
Telephone: 802-226-7770
Rooms: Seven, one with private bath.
Rates: $38 to $42, per person, MAP.
Facilities: Open all year. Breakfast and dinner. Beer and wine
   license. Golf, tennis, bicycling, skiing, and skating near-
   by. All major credit cards accepted.

The first thing you notice when you enter the inn is a
monster of a spinning wheel in the front hall. In the living
room there is an exquisite old pump organ. This room is all
comfort, armchairs, couches, a crackling fire to warm your
toes, and an enticing chaise in front of a sunny bay window.

All of the guest rooms are attractive, and one has a
lovely, eyelet-canopied bed.

Joan is "chief cook and bottle washer." The aromas
of ☛ freshly baked bread, freshly perked coffee, and home-
smoked bacon will awaken you. If you have a special occasion a ☛ champagne breakfast in bed is a nice treat.

There is so much to do in this area year round. Spring is the time to watch the maple sugaring or just go fishing in one of the well-stocked lakes or streams. In summer golf, tennis, hiking, and bicycling are close at hand. Fall is foliage and cider. Winter brings the skiing and skating, or you could also curl up with a good book by the fire.

How to get there: Take I-91 to Exit 6 in Bellows Falls. Go north on Route 103 to its junction with Route 131 and turn right. The inn is on the left in a quarter of a mile.

E: *Tumble in the Rumble, as it says in their brochure. In good weather a ride in the ▬ rumble seat of a 1935 Plymouth complete with a raccoon coat on the driver and assorted appropriate coats for the guests is my kind of fun.*

Spring flowers add the final brush strokes
at the edges of the granite walk
to the inn's front stoop.

The Quechee Inn
Quechee, Vermont
05059

Innkeepers: Michael and Barbara Yaroschuk
Telephone: 802-295-3133
Rooms: 22, all with private bath and TV.
Rates: $60 to $125, double occupancy, continental breakfast
   included.
Facilities: Closed three weeks in December and most of April.
   Breakfast, dinner Wednesday through Sunday, bar.
   Antique shop. Cross-country and downhill skiing, golf,
   tennis, swimming, boating, fishing, and hiking. Master-
   Card and Visa accepted.

The first time I saw and heard Quechee Gorge I was
standing on the bridge that spans it. Now I know another
way to see this remarkable quirk of nature. The inn is but
one-half mile from it, and ☛ the innkeepers will show you
how to see it from an unusual angle.

Quechee Inn was a private home from 1793 until 1976.
Beautifully converted to an inn, it reflects the care the innkeepers give it. Some of the rooms have the largest ☛ four-

poster, king-sized beds I have ever seen, others have twins, and all are equipped with cable color TV.

A new wing houses the kitchen, dining room, and seven more guest rooms with picture windows overlooking the meadow and lake. Adjoining the dining room is a small library and conference room wired for audio-visual equipment. It's a real treat to be able to have a business meeting at a place like this. The living room has an abundance of comfortable couches and chairs, a piano, color TV, books, and a fireplace. One feels at home here any season of the year.

The inn guests have ☛ full club privileges at the Quechee Club. The golf courses are breathtakingly scenic and are great tests of golf. If you do intend to play, let the inn know when you call for reservations so they can arrange a tee off time for you.

New additions to this lovely spot are a golden retriever named Governor Marsh, and an antique shop in the barn.

How to get there: From I-91 take Route 89 north to Exit 1. Go west on Route 4 for 1.2 miles, then right on Club House Road for one mile to the inn.

🍶

E: *Old-fashioned New England dining with homemade breads,* ☛ *sticky buns, and regional specials such as trout and venison make a visit here a must.*

Saxtons River Inn
Saxtons River, Vermont
05154

Innkeepers: The Campbell Family, Averill Campbell Larsen
Telephone: 802-869-2110
Rooms: 15, six with private bath; five suites in Colvin House
across the street.
Rates: $27.50 to $55, double occupancy, continental breakfast included.
Facilities: Closed January through March. Dinner, Sunday
brunch, bar. No credit cards honored, but personal
checks accepted.

Blessings on the Campbell family, and especially on
Averill Campbell, who was responsible for renovating this
turn-of-the-century inn and revitalizing the little village of
Saxtons River. ☞ Cross the wide front porch and come
through the gracious front door. To the right is a little breakfast room, to the left, the copper bar. Straight ahead is the
dining room. Tiffany chandeliers light the flower-bedecked
tables, and some of the freshest, most original food is brought
out from the spick-and-span kitchen to please even the most

particular diner.

☛ The guest rooms are spectacular, handsomely decorated with a combination of old furniture and crisp new fabrics. Your innkeeper has traveled around the world and knows what is needed for creature comforts, including pleasant places to read, with lights in the right places. She has slept in every one of her guest rooms, an acid test, and she has her own aerie at the top of the tower, five stories above the world of Saxtons River.

The menu changes, of course, with what is fresh and good in season. If you are really not hungry you can have soup and salad for a most nominal price. If you are starving, begin with soup or Mushroom Maison, Rumaki, or Ratatouille, and go on to a main course of steak, Chicken Louise, or Cocquille St. Jacques. But be sure to save room for dessert. They all are appallingly good, and are outlawed by every diet-club in the country.

How to get there: From I-91 take either Exit 5 or 6 at Bellows Falls. Pick up Route 5, and proceed to Route 121. Saxtons River is on Route 121, and the inn is on Main Street in the center of town.

E: *I love to read in bed, and this is the most comfortable place for doing it.*

*Hark, which are common noises
and which are the ghosts of long contented guests.*

Olive Metcalf

The Londonderry Inn
South Londonderry, Vermont
05155

Innkeepers: Jim and Jean Cavanagh
Telephone: 802-824-5226
Rooms: 25, 22 with private bath.
Rates: $32 to $54.50, double occupancy, EPB.
Facilities: Inn open all year. Restaurant closed late October to mid-December, and April to late May. Lunch summer and fall, dinner, bar. Pool tables, Ping-Pong, swimming. Skiing, horseback riding, and hiking nearby. No credit cards honored, but personal checks accepted.

The inn sits high on a hill overlooking the village of South Londonderry. It is central to three big ski areas, Bromley, Magic Mountain, and Stratton.

In summer there is a large heated swimming pool. Nearby they have horseback riding, hiking, and bicycle trails. Any time of the year there is pool to be played on the inn's two ☛ vintage pool tables. In addition, there are many comfortable places to relax, read a book, do needlepoint, or just enjoy a blazing fire on the hearth.

The inn dates back to 1826 when it was a farmhouse. The rooms have twin, double, and king-sized beds with ☞ down comforters, ☞ down pillows, and large thirsty towels. Jean also puts ☞ fresh flowers in the rooms. These little touches are far too often overlooked by innkeepers.

The inn has a nice lounge and a service bar off the living room, so you can be comfortable by the fire before dinner with your favorite cocktail in hand. The menu changes nightly, but always includes four to eight entrees served with fresh vegetables, four or five appetizers, at least one home-made soup, and great desserts.

Honey is the inn dog you will love.

How to get there: Take Exit 2 from I-91 at Brattleboro, and follow Route 30 north to Rawsonville. Then take Route 100 to South Londonderry. The inn is on your left.

E: *The dessert names are really creative, FBI Cake, Orient Express Torte, and Hungarian Rhapsody.*

If you have never been drawn shivering
from the warmth of a good bed
by the sizzling lure of bacon on the grill,
you have never been in a country inn.

Charda
Stowe, Vermont
05672

Innkeepers: Julius and Trudy Tarlo
Telephone: 802-253-4598
Rooms: 11, all with private bath.
Rates: In summer, $22; in winter, $34; double occupancy;
EPB.
Facilities: Closed from Thanksgiving to Christmas, and mid-
April to Memorial Day. Dinner, bar. Ramps available for
wheelchairs in dining room. No credit cards accepted.

Charda looks as if it belongs in the Alps, though it comes
complete with the charm and food of a fine Hungarian
restaurant. The inn has a splendid view of Mount Mansfield
and Spruce Peak. ☛ The old barn was turned into rooms,
and believe me, the Tarlos have done a fine job. Some rooms
have a double bed and a twin, and all have private baths for a
very comfortable stay.
☛ Hungarian food at its best is served here, featuring
favorites like stuffed cabbage, Kasseler Rippchen, smoked
loin of pork with sauerkraut, Hungarian beef goulash, and

Wiener Bachendle, which is a boneless breast of chicken prepared like a schnitzel with rice and mushrooms. The desserts, to name but a few, include chestnut purée topped with whipped cream, Kahlua, and chocolate sprinkles; cheesecake with black cherries in a rum topping; and more, if you forget your diet.

The small bar in the center of this lovely dining room has an espresso and cappuccino machine that turns out heavenly coffees. Converted oil lamps hang from the ceiling of the dining room and from the windows, which have stained glass in them. You can look out at the magnificent mountain range as you sit here. The wine list is unusual, with many selections from Hungary, Austria, and Germany. And, of course, there are good imported beers.

One more note on desserts: they have Palacsinta. You must go and find out about this one for yourself.

How to get there: Take I-89 to Route 100 and go north. The inn is on the left, north of Stowe.

E: *The inn cat is a beauty of a calico named Malisa.*

Innkeeping takes twenty-five hours
of every twenty-four, but done right
it makes a wonderful life.

Edson Hill Manor
Stowe, Vermont
05672

Innkeepers: The Heath Family
Telephone: 802-253-7371, 802-253-9797
Rooms: 15, 11 with seven baths in manor, four with 2 baths in annex; some suites.
Rates: $48 to $65, per person, MAP.
Facilities: Closed in November, and mid-May to mid-June. Breakfast, lunch in winter only, dinner, fully licensed bar, après-ski lounge. Pool, fishing, horseback riding and instruction, cross-country skiing with rentals and instruction. Ice-skating and golf at Stowe Country Club nearby. No credit cards honored, but personal checks accepted.

Here you are, halfway between Stowe and Mount Mansfield, 1500 feet above the hubble-bubble of that lively village of Stowe that is growing every year. Here is truly luxurious living, in a house that was built in 1939 for a family that loved to ski and ride.

☛ The swimming pool here is beautiful. It won an

award from Paddock Pools of California. The stocked trout pond is a must for anglers. When the snow comes, the stables turn into a cross-country ski center, so there you are, practically taking off from the inn door.

This attractive house has been run as an inn since 1953, and there are still homelike touches. The pine paneled living room has an aura of quiet elegance that reflects the feeling of gracious living all too often missing from our busy lives.

Downstairs are bar and lounge. A skier's lunch is served here. Hot soup of the day, chef's salad, hot chili, and good sandwiches. A special on cold days is hot mulled cider.

This is a beautiful inn. Many of the paintings were done by Effie Juraine Martin Heath, the grandmother of the family. The view is spectacular, and Bow, the inn's golden retriever, is a must-see beauty.

A note of particular interest to all you moviegoers is that Edson Hill Manor was the winter filming location for Alan Alda's "The Four Seasons."

There are so many different rates and packages for so many different activities, I suggest you write for the complete set of brochures.

How to get there: Take Route 108 north from Stowe 4.9 miles, turn right on Edson Hill Road, and follow the signs, uphill, to the Manor.

E: *The old Delft tiles around many of the fireplaces are so appealing. Look closely at the living room curtains. Somebody shopped hard for that material.*

Foxfire Inn
Stowe, Vermont
05672

Innkeepers: Irene and Art Segreto
Telephone: 802-253-4887
Rooms: Five, all with private bath; chalets.
Rates: $36 to $44, double occupancy, EP; or, $76 to $84, double occupancy, MAP.
Facilities: Open all year. Breakfast, dinner, bar. Parking. Downhill and cross-country skiing, fishing, skating, and hiking nearby. American Express, MasterCard, and Visa accepted.

The Segretos want to welcome old and new friends, and there are myriads of them, to their inn. The house is over 150 years old and has been restored to easy comfort by these enthusiastic innkeepers. And there is so much to do here, from the finest skiing in the East to great lounging by the pool.

There is a beautiful inn dog, Coby, a "formerly white" Samoyed who smiles his secret smile to greet you. Irene says he is just impossible to keep clean, but he did not look that dingy to me. Could be the contrast with the snow.

Irene has created a garden room that is a great spot for lunch. It is all white lattice with loads of hanging plants. This is a gazebo to end them all.

The best Italian kitchen in New England may seem a bit misplaced so far north in Vermont, but it is here. Taste, and you will agree. The tomato sauce is an old family recipe brought over from Naples. And do try things like Baked Broccoli, which is a combination of tomato sauce, ricotta cheese, and broccoli. There are seven different and delicious veal dishes. Boneless breast of chicken is prepared five ways, and the Eggplant Parmigiana has a special place in my heart. Shrimp Marinara I can still taste. As the front of the menu says, here you discover "The Italian Art of Eating."

And when you can push yourself away from the table, you have Stowe at your door, with antiques, shops, skiing, skating, walking, hiking, fishing, and more.

How to get there: Take I-89 to Route 100 north into Stowe. The inn is on the right, 1½ miles north of town.

♚

E: *Pass me another tortoni, please. I am settled in for the season.*

*A cricket on the hearth of a country inn
is music beyond the angels.*

205

Spruce Pond Inn
Stowe, Vermont
05672

Innkeepers: Max and Margaret Holland
Telephone: 802-253-4828
Rooms: 16, all with private bath and air conditioning.
Rates: $35 to $60, double occupancy, EP.
Facilities: Closed from Easter to May 15, and October 20 to December 1. Breakfast, dinner, bar. Game house. Skiing, hiking, biking, and skating nearby. All major credit cards accepted.

The first thing you see when you enter the inn is a coat rack of a black bear and three cubs from the Black Forest in Germany. Stroll down the brick walkway, which is full of plants, and you pass by a very unusual grandfather's clock, oriental in style. In ☛ 1740 it went from England to China for its beautiful engraving, then was shipped back to England, and now it lives here.

The bar-lounge is a wonderful place to unwind after skiing, hiking, biking, or whatever you do. It is a very comfortable bar with chairs, couches, and a large stone fireplace.

The living room also has a huge fireplace and generous couches and chairs. All in all, wherever you decide to relax, you'll be more than comfortable.

Food here is excellent. The menu is expansive. A few of the goodies are Broiled King Crab Legs, Chicken Chasseur, and Veal Oscar. Other treats are their flambé dishes cooked at your table. A fine wine cellar makes it all go together.

Stowe is a skier's paradise; Mount Mansfield and Spruce Peak offer the best skiing in the East. Cross-country buffs have miles of trails. Others can enjoy tobogganing, skating, and country sleigh rides.

For children "The Old Milk House" is a delightful recreation spot. It is adjacent to the inn and has games for the whole family.

The animals are fun. Joe Stowe is a Yorkie, Daisy, a tomcat, and Lilly, a white goat.

How to get there: Take I-89 to Route 100 north. The inn is on the left going into town.

E: *A swim in the spring-fed pond is for the brave, but between shivers the view is superb.*

A country inn piled high with snow is a cheery fortress against the cold.

olive Metcalf

Echo Lake Inn Resort
Tyson, Vermont
(Mailing address: P. O. Box 154, Ludlow, VT 05149)

Innkeepers: Mark and Jo Brown
Telephone: 802-228-8602
Rooms: 20, four with private bath; five family units.
Rates: $15 to $24, per person, EP.
Facilities: Closed first two weeks in April. Breakfast, lunch in summer and fall, dinner. Lounge, game room. Tennis, heated swimming pool, lake, boating, cross-country skiing. Downhill skiing, fishing, golf, and horseback riding nearby. American Express, MasterCard, and Visa accepted.

Echo Lake is an authentic "old Colonial inn" that has been welcoming travelers for 175 years. The inn has been completely restored and modernized, including 🖙 an automatic fire alarm system, but its charm has been retained; hence their slogan, "The charm of old Vermont."

For your comfort you may relax in one of the exquisitely appointed bedrooms. The family units are perfect for large skiing or hiking groups, or a family.

All meals are prepared by two fully certified chefs. They serve marvelous food. From fish, fresh daily, to the chef's specials, which range from chicken, roasts, steaks, and chops, there is something for everyone here; and it always can be topped off with the fruit pies that are made daily.

For your enjoyment the inn's living room, with a cheery fireplace, is perfect for a game of cards, reading, playing the piano, watching TV, or just relaxing. There is a large, heated swimming pool with a bathhouse and shower facilities. And the sandy beach on Echo Lake is but 100 yards from the inn. The inn has rowboats, canoes, and sailboats for you to enjoy. Echo is the middle lake of the three-stream, spring-fed Plymouth Lakes.

A nice touch at the inn are the all-weather tennis courts, lighted for nighttime play. And for you winter buffs, the skiing season is long up here in northern Vermont. There are six good alpine areas nearby, and cross-country skiing right on the inn's property.

How to get there: From I-91 take Exit 6 to Route 103 to Ludlow. Turn right on Route 100 1½ miles north of Ludlow. The inn is 4 miles up the road.

☼

E: *The lakes mirror the brilliant colors of fall like nowhere else in New England. Spectacular!*

The cheers of millions are for politicians,
while the quiet appreciation of a well cooked chop
is but for a few.

Tucker Hill Lodge
Waitsfield, Vermont
05673

Innkeepers: Emily and Zeke Church; Carter Parkinson
Telephone: 802-496-3983
Rooms: 20, 14 with private bath.
Rates: $39 to $49, per person, double occupancy, MAP.
Facilities: Open all year. Dinner served in season. Sunday
brunch only through October, cross-country lunches,
bar. Swimming pool. Skiing, fishing, tennis, and golf
nearby. All major credit cards accepted.

You will find Tucker Hill Lodge nestled on a wooded
ridge overlooking the road that winds up to the Mad River
Glen Ski Area. ☛ Route 17, by the way, is one of the most
spectacular roads you will ever find.

The inn is cozy, ☛ fresh flowers in your room, handmade quilts on most of the beds, comfortable living rooms
and caring innkeepers.

The menu changes every day, and the food is excellent,
with inventive dishes like shrimp and watercress salad with a
vinaigrette gourmande dressing, or avocado and grapefruit

salad with a dressing of grapefruit and lemon juices, scallions, and olive oil. The veal is tender and light. One way it is served is with asparagus sauce, another is with lemon sabayon sauce. I like the different touches the chef has up here. They also serve interesting fish dishes like poached tile fish with shrimp and leeks, or poached monk fish with a tomato beurre blanc sauce. Of course, beef and chicken are on the menu too. And would you believe a coffee called Dastardly Mash? Come on up and try it.

There is a lot doing up here, tennis, skiing, of course, and a Robert Trent Jones golf course nearby. There is plenty of fishing or just relaxing in this lovely inn. Do remember to pat Blue, the inn dog.

How to get there: Turn west off Route 100 onto Route 7 in Waitsfield in the Mad River Valley. Go 1½ miles west; the sign for the lodge will be on your left.

E: *I cannot think of a nicer place to sit than on the deck, under the trees, sipping something long and cool, or I'll take the menu, one item at a time, from Tabouli, Seviche, to Roast Pork with Mustard sauce. Yum, yum.*

To find a good inn as darkness glowers on the horizon, there is no treasure to match it.

Olive Metcalf

The Wallingford Inn
Wallingford, Vermont
05773

Innkeepers: Al Bruce and Kathy Knowlton
Telephone: 802-446-2849
Rooms: Six, all with private bath.
Rates: $35 to $48, double occupancy, continental breakfast
   included.
Facilities: Closed Mondays and first two weeks in November.
   Dinner, bar. Banquet facilities. No pets. Fishing, skiing,
   and other sports nearby. MasterCard and Visa accepted.

The inn is a beautifully restored Victorian mansion built
in 1876. It is also an 🐕 in-town inn. This is a nice change
from the country, allowing you to stroll down the tree-lined
streets of Wallingford. There are nice things to do in this area.
The Battenkill River has good fishing. There are covered
bridges, antique shops, and at hand is The Green Mountain
National Forest, a photographer's paradise in every season.
Winter brings cross-country skiing, and, indeed, all the other
winter sports.

There are three dining rooms at the inn. One of them is

done in my favorite colors, blue and white. All of the good food is prepared to your order, which is the only way to eat. The inn is famous for its Caesar salad. All entrees are served with this salad. The scallops are a little different, broiled with bacon bits and shallots. The trout is boneless, a nice touch. They also have some Italian specials each day.The after-dinner delights (the words are from their brochure) are just that, nine different parfaits, homemade Key lime pie, hot apple pie, and more and more and more.

The inn is delightful, with high ceilings, fireplaces, lovely chandeliers, polished wood floors, and elegant wood-work. There are six rooms and all have their own baths. There is a nice bar and lounge. Look for the green dragon on the bar. Unique.

How to get there: The inn is about 20 minutes south of Rutland on the Western side of Route 7 in Wallingford. It is 9 North Main Street.

E: *The blue room with the antique four-poster bed is glorious.*

The Inn at Weathersfield
Weathersfield, Vermont
05151

Innkeepers: Mary Louise and Ron Thorburn
Telephone: 802-263-9217
Rooms: 12, ten with private bath; one suite.
Rates: $32 per person, double occupancy, EPB plus afternoon
high tea; or, $50 per person, double occupancy, MAP
and tea.
Facilities: Open all year. Breakfast, dinner, high tea. Service
bar. Library, horse and carriage stalls. MasterCard and
Visa accepted.

This beautiful old inn was built circa 1776 and has a
wonderful history. At one point in the Civil War it was an
important stop on the underground railroad, hiding slaves
en route to Canada. The inn is set well back from the road.
Your rest is assured.

The rooms are beautiful, with ☛ fresh flowers, fresh
fruit, canopy beds, electric sheets, ☛ feathered pillows,
stencilled walls. At night your bed is turned down and a
candy placed on your pillow.

☛ Breakfast, complete with freshly squeezed orange juice, is served in your room. The dining room, once the carriage house, has a good part of its walls lined with books, and above the books a fascinating bottle collection. The innkeepers are both accomplished musicians and can be persuaded to play. Ron played the piano for me while I had lunch. He has a nice touch on the keys. The food is imaginative and different. ☛ Cider jelly is made nearby and used in some cooking. I never had had it before, so I bought some and used it as a baste on lamb chops at home. Delicious! Chicken Weathersfield is just one of Mary Louise's recipes that does wonderful things with boneless breast of chicken.

The inn has many mulberry trees from which the owners make a sweet and sour mulberry sauce, one use for which is on stuffed pork chops. The beautiful silver serving pieces are functional as well as decorative. To make all things work just right, Ron has an ☛ extensive and good wine cellar.

Daughter Heather and husband, Jack, are potters. Their fine work is used in the inn, and certain pieces are for sale here.

How to get there: Exit 7 from I-91. Take Route 106 north to Perkinsville. About one-half mile short of the village you will find the inn on your left set well back from the road.

☖

E: *A wassail cup is served from a cauldron in the keeping room fireplace. High tea is a special I love along with a gaggle of inn dogs known as ''Mom's Moldy Muppets.''*

Olive Metcalf

Grandmother's House
West Arlington, Vermont
05250

Innkeeper: Mrs. Walter Finney
Telephone: 802-375-2328
Rooms: Five, three double, two single, with two and one-half
   baths.
Rates: $45 per person, MAP. Reservations and deposit re-
   quired. Mrs. Finney really likes you to stay at least two
   nights.
Facilities: Open all year. Breakfast, dinner, no bar. Parking.
   Fishing and tennis. Near skiing. No credit cards accepted.

Of course you must go over the river and through the
covered bridge to reach Grandmother's House. When you
arrive, you may find a hand-lettered sign on the door saying,
"Grandmother Washing Hair. Holler loudly." Mrs. Finney,
official Grandmother to the world, has a whole file of signs
for any occasion. She prefers her guests to stay more than
one night. If you stay awhile, you can really begin to relax.
   ☛ This is a superb place for fishermen. Don't ask
about antique shops, Mrs. Finney doesn't go to them. Her

216

house is filled with beautiful things, and one of her prizes is a tiger maple four-poster, made by her (we think) great, great grandfather.

Loaf under the great shady maples, play tennis, croquet, or horseshoes, take long walks along country lanes, or ski in winter. Once upon a time Norman Rockwell, the artist, lived in this house, and you are right across the lane from a dear little Methodist church.

How to get there: Turn off Route 7 in Arlington onto Route 313. Go 4 miles to a covered bridge on the left, and cross that bridge to Grandmother's House. Or, take Route 22 from Cambridge, New York to Route 313. Go 12 miles, and the covered bridge will be on your right.

E: Look at the figures holding the plants on each side of the porch. They came from Mrs Finney's grandmother's conservatory. They are charming.

I have enjoyed the hospitality of a good inn
and I am ready for the day ahead.

217

The Inn at Sawmill Farm
West Dover, Vermont
05356

Innkeepers: Rodney, Brill, and Ione Williams
Telephone: 802-464-8131
Rooms: 22, all with private bath.
Rates: $120 to $180, double occupancy, MAP; in foliage
season and between Christmas and New Year's Day, $10
higher.
Facilities: Closed Sunday after Thanksgiving to mid-December. Dinner, bar, lounge. Swimming pool, tennis, 2½-acre trout fishing pond. No credit cards accepted.

The Williams have transformed an old Vermont barn into the gayest, warmest, most attractive inn that I have seen in many a country mile. Ione is a professional decorator and Rod is an architect, which makes for a wonderful marriage of talents for a just perfect inn, indoors and out.

Gardens greet you as you drive up, and once inside you will find lots of barn siding cleverly used with interesting antique farm implements hung thereon. The copper collection around the ☞ oversized fireplace is a sight to see, and the huge copper-topped coffee table nearby is a beauty. The library is an old hayloft over the end of the living room, and a majestic place for the solitary reader.

The Pot Belly Lounge has an incredible bar of solid copper. It also houses the Williams' collection of ancient ice skates, biscuit tins, and a player piano that really works. Beyond the bar is an enclosed porch that contains a small greenhouse. When I was there this spring it was full of passion flowers and bougainvillea, and is a very nice spot to enjoy the wonderful food that is served.

The Williams' son, Brill, runs the kitchen. Ione does the pies. Both are fussy and excellent cooks. What a nice family combination for the inn business.

Accommodations are very different, with some Victorian rooms, some done in Chippendale, and all with the flavor of New England at its best. A few suites have fireplaces, and my favorite is the Cider House. All are color-coordinated with thick towels and extra pillows. And as a final touch fresh fruit is served in your room.

How to get there: Take I-91 to Exit 2 in Brattleboro. Take Route 9 west to Wilmington, and then follow Route 100 north 6 miles to West Dover.

E: *The inn makes a special of special times. Do try to get up here for Christmas. It's something you will never forget.*

Olive Metcalf

Snow Den Inn
West Dover, Vermont
05356

Innkeepers: Milt and Jean Cummings
Telephone: 802-464-5537
Rooms: Ten, eight with private bath.
Rates: $40 to $45, double occupancy, EP. Special package
   plans available in winter.
Facilities: Open all year. Breakfast, lunch in summer, dinner
   in winter. BYOB. All summer and winter sports nearby.
   All major credit cards accepted.

Snow Den is a nice name for an inn up here in snow
country. There is so much to keep you busy and happy in this
area. The inn is two miles from Mount Snow and two minutes from the Mount Snow Golf Course. Skiing, snowmobiling, cross-country skiing, and all sorts of other season activities are also at hand.

The inn is informal and comfortable. The den is large,
has a fireplace, and a picture window that overlooks Mount
Snow. A good place to relax after a day's activities. The

bedrooms are large. ☞ One is done in my favorite color, blue.

Milt is the chef. One entree is served each night. Some friends reported that breakfast was yummy, French toast, eggs, crisp bacon, and homemade zucchini nut bread.

And to make things warm and wonderful, there is a nice wood stove in the dining room.

How to get there: Take Route I-91 to Brattleboro. Take Route 9 west to Wilmington, and then follow Route 100 about 5 miles to West Dover. The inn is on your right in the middle of the village.

🗑

E: *The inn was built in 1885 and was the first ski lodge at Mount Snow.*

> *"Does the road wind uphill all the way?*
> *Yes, to the very end.*
> *Will the day's journey take the whole day long?*
> *From morn to night, my friend."*
> —Christina Rossetti

Olive Metcalf

The Weathervane Lodge
West Dover, Vermont
05356

Innkeepers: Liz and Ernie Chabot
Telephone: 802-464-5426
Rooms: Ten, four with private bath; one suite; one apartment.
Rates: $17 to $27, per person, double occupancy, EPB; in winter, $25 to $44, per person, double occupancy, MAP.
Facilities: Open all year. Breakfast, dinner in ski season, BYOB bar. Lounge. Near skiing and other sports. No credit cards accepted.

When I drove in the parking lot of the Weathervane I met the inn cat, Spooky, sleeping under a car. Cesar, the loveable shepherd, gave a small woof.

This is a family inn that ☛ never closes. It is warmly furnished with authentic antiques and has tons of Colonial charm. One of the suites might suit your family rather well. It has two bedrooms, a kitchen, and a living room with a fireplace.

Dinner is served during the ski season only, and breakfast is served year round. There is a variety of restaurants in the area to choose from in the off seasons.

The lounge and recreation room have a set-up bar where you bring your own bottle, enjoy the fireplace, piano, play Ping-Pong, and have fun.

There is much to do here all seasons, but do remember that this is a family inn, not as fancy as some, but a good place for a relaxing few days.

How to get there: From Wilmington take Route 100 north to West Dover. The inn is on the Dorr Fitch Road.

⚖

E: *I like keeping things in the family, especially as in this case, when it was the inn. The son of this inn's family married the daughter of the innkeepers of On the Rocks Inn.*

For one night at least
let me escape from all those things
the Puritans tell me I must face.
Let me find a friendly inn.

West Dover Inn
West Dover, Vermont
05356

Innkeepers: Alice O'Toole, Walter and Joan Rosenthal
Telephone: 802-464-5207
Rooms: 12, two with private bath.
Rates: $35 to $45, double occupancy, EP.
Facilities: Open all year. Breakfast, dinner, full service bar. TV
   in sitting room. Skiing, golf, tennis, horseback riding,
   boating, and swimming nearby. American Express,
   MasterCard, and Visa accepted.

Alice O'Toole and the Rosenthals have owned the West
Dover Inn for several years. I've always believed we need
inns for all sorts of people. This is a perfect inn for visits by
full families. It is a warm, nice inn, not fancy, but good.
   The food served here also is good. The inn special is
☛ Baked Seafood Supreme: clams, shrimp, and crabmeat
baked with real cream and topped with parmesan cheese.
Yum, yum. Fresh spinach salad, good soups, and lots more to
go with the special of the day are also offered.
   There is a wealth of things to do in this area of Vermont

every season of the year. For winter you have skiing, both cross-country and Alpine. For the warmer months you have golf, tennis, horseback riding, hiking, and walking. Boats and canoes are on Lake Whitingham which is 12 miles away. Nearby lakes provide swimming. Vermont is beautiful to see and to play in, so come and enjoy.

How to get there: Take Exit 2 from I-91 at Brattleboro, Vermont, then take Route 9 west to Route 100 north. In West Dover you will find the inn on your right in the village.

E: *The magnificent old piano in the parlor is a dream.*

*Let us escape for a day, or better a week,
and hide away in a country inn.*

Olive Metcalf

The Inn at Weston
Weston, Vermont
05161

Innkeepers: Stu and Sue Douglas
Telephone: 802-824-5804
Rooms: 13, six with private bath.
Rates: $38 to $46, per person, MAP.
Facilities: Closed November, and mid-April to mid-May. Dining room closed Wednesdays. Breakfast, lunch in winter on Saturdays, dinner, Sunday brunch, bar. TV, fireplace in lounge. Wheelchair ramp available for dining room and one ground floor bedroom. Skiing nearby. No credit cards accepted.

If you walk in the front door of this lovely inn, you are in Sue Douglas' kitchen, and Sue is the chef. She greets you with a warm smile and great culinary treats. The weekend I was here, the fare was ☛ Poached Salmon with Mustard Sauce, Roast Beef, Chicken Kiev, and a Greek dinner salad. There is a different dinner salad served each night.

Stu is the breakfast chef, and he makes marvelous ☛ whole wheat, cornmeal, and rye pancakes, or French toast made from Sue's homemade breads. It is all served with Vermont bacon and maple syrup. The homemade apple butter contains ☞ whole slices of apple, and the blueberry muffins are so good.

The rooms are small, and very very pleasant with old antique beds that are comfortable. The dining room has so much charm and warmth, with walls of real barn siding, and everyone who works here ☞ smiles. They are a happy group.

Weston is the home of the Vermont Country Store. It is a short stroll down the road, and a mecca for browsers. The inn is close to several ski areas, so do come and enjoy. As the Douglases say, "This is where friendships begin," and they really do. If you are on a special diet, tell Sue and she will try to help you stay within it.

How to get there: Off I-91, on Exit 6, take Route 103 to Chester. Follow Route 11 to Londonderry, and turn right on Route 100 to Weston. The inn is in the Village.

E: *Afternoon tea is served at 4, with hot spiced cider and Sue's homemade goodies—Wow!*

> *To eat merely to live*
> *is a crime against man*
> *for which the gibbet is*
> *inadequate punishment.*

Windham Hill Inn
West Townshend, Vermont
05359

Innkeepers: Linda and Ken Busteed
Telephone: 802-874-4080
Rooms: Ten, eight with private bath.
Rates: $43 to $45, per person, double occupancy, MAP.
Facilities: Open all year. Breakfast, dinner, full license. All the
activities of all seasons. MasterCard and Visa.

At Windham Hill Inn you are sitting on the top of the
world. It is beautiful up here. The West River Valley stretches
as far as the eye can see. Built originally about 1825, it was a
working dairy farm, and in 1962 was converted into an inn
which it has remained.

The family-style meals are memorable. Linda is the
chef, and she makes all her own 🖝 breads and desserts as
well as her soups and appetizers. Ken is the breakfast chef,
and together this pair make a great team. In season all the
vegetables are fresh, most from the inn's gardens.

The rooms are charming, with 🖝 two of them having
their own balconies. The living room is full of Victorian

wicker and has a good New England wood stove. Off of this is a lovely balcony that overlooks the world. The whole inn feels like home. There are plants everywhere. I found a large stack of old LIFE magazines, something I love. They also have a well-stocked library.

There is much to do here, a practice ski slope, floodlit ice-skating pond, tobogganing, sledding, snowshoeing, and cross-country skiing. Nearby are Stratton Mountain, Big Bromley, Magic Mountain, Mount Snow, Snow Valley, Maple Valley, and Timber Ridge. A schuss-boomers dream come true.

How to get there: Take Exit 2 off I-91 in Brattleboro, then Route 30 for 21 miles to West Townshend. At the Country Store turn right, up the hill, onto Windham Road. Look for the inn's sign on the right in 1½ miles.

⊕

E: *The peonies were in bloom. They have some in two colors. Another garden sight I had never seen before was their magnificent Fringe tree.*

Brook Bound
Wilmington, Vermont
05363

Innkeepers: The Fajans
Telephone: 802-464-5267
Rooms: Nine, five with private bath; two housekeeping
  chalets.
Rates: $27 to $35, per person, MAP.
Facilities: Closed mid-October to mid-December, and mid-
  April to mid-June. Breakfast, dinner. BYOB, setups pro-
  vided. Recreation room, pool table, Ping-Pong, swim-
  ming, tennis. Music and skiing nearby. No credit cards
  accepted.

"In the beautiful Green Mountains of southern Vermont, off a country road in a lovely quiet setting with commanding views of Haystack and Mount Snow, there is this
warm and friendly inn waiting to welcome you." This is a
quote from the inn's brochure, and it is so well said.

The grounds are spacious, and the ☛ pool is heated. It
sits up above the inn with the tennis courts beyond. There

230

are glorious big trees all over, and in the fall they are a sight to behold.

Food here is served family-style, with much of it home-grown. Set-ups are provided for your drink, and in the winter it all happens around a neat fireplace. The inn has a refrigerator especially for guests to keep luncheon food and snacks or drinks. This is a nice thing to do.

Two chalets are close by. The smaller one holds up to six people and the larger one can accommodate 11. You do your own cooking and housekeeping.

The inn is close to several ski areas for both downhill and cross-country skiing. There is so much to do in this area any season of the year that it would take pages just to list everything.

You are only 12 miles from the Marlboro Music Festival or the Brattleboro Music Center's Bach program. A real turn-on for a music lover.

How to get there: From Wilmington take Route 100 north and turn left on Cold Brook Road. Go 2.2 miles to the inn.

E: *Animals again. Heather is a lovely collie and there is a cat, a cat by the name of Zipper. They also breed, train, and board Morgan horses.*

A warming fire, a strong drink, a genial innkeeper . . . and winter is somewhere in the hills but is not here.

Olive Metcalf

The Hermitage
Wilmington, Vermont
05363

Innkeeper: James McGovern
Telephone: 802-464-3759
Rooms: 16, all with private bath, 11 with fireplace.
Rates: $60 to $70, per person, double occupancy, MAP.
Facilities: Open all year. Lunch in season, dinner. Sauna,
      wine cellar. Cross-country skiing from inn door, hiking,
      trout pond, tennis, game bird farm. Accessible to
      wheelchairs. All major credit cards accepted.

High on a windy hill facing Haystack Mountain, you
will find a unique and heartwarming country inn, The Hermitage. The owner is a man for all seasons who knows what
he is doing. He also has a certain charm, maybe it is the quick
smile or a fleeting twinkle as he says, ☞ "No piped-in music
in *my* inn." You might, though, find a classical guitarist some
night, or someone at the piano in the lounge.

Come in the very early spring, and you will find maple
sugaring going full blast. There are four sugarhouses on the
property, and Jim McGovern makes 700 gallons of maple

syrup in an unexceptional year. In summer the big kettles are kept simmering, making homemade jams and jellies. Along with this talent for making the most of nature's bounty, Jim is an oenophile (wine lover), and has a 🐖 wine cellar with a stock of 30,000 bottles. You are never at a loss for the perfect wine to enjoy with this inn's first-rate food.

There are four separate dining rooms. No more than 20 people can be accommodated in each room, so there is a feeling of intimacy, each place providing for quiet conversation while you enjoy a beautiful dinner. The Vermont marble terrace with its gay umbrellas is the right spot for a bit of lunch. The fruit and cheese plate couldn't be better, with five kinds of excellent cheese and five fresh fruits. Cognac and Burgundy, two friendly English setters, may come by to say hello, but they are likely to be distracted by a passing gaggle of geese which *will* fly off in a flurry of wings.

The comfortable rooms, 11 with their own fireplaces, are furnished with antiques and, oh, those brass beds. In the carriage house you will even find a sauna.

How to get there: Take Route 9 to Wilmington, follow Route 100 north 2 miles to Coldbrook Road on the left. The Hermitage is 3 miles down Coldbrook Road.

☿

E: *The wine cellar, with its two crystal chandeliers, marvelous selection of wine and gifts, turned me on. What to do with your old claw-footed bathtub? Use it to store wine. There is also an old bassinet used for the same purpose.*

Nutmeg Inn
Wilmington, Vermont
05363

Innkeepers: Joan and Rich Combes
Telephone: 802-464-3351
Rooms: Nine, four with private bath.
Rates: In summer and fall, $42 to $55, double occupancy,
EPB; in winter, $34 to $45, per person, MAP.
Facilities: Closed November to December 26, April and May.
Dinner in winter only, many restaurants nearby. BYOB
bar. Tennis. Near music, skiing, and golf. No pets. No
children under nine. No credit cards accepted.

Wilmington has quite a few country inns, and nice
ones. It is understandable, with so many lovely old houses
placed here and there through the village and hills.

The Nutmeg was originally an early American Vermont
farmhouse. In 1957 the farmhouse was taken over, restored
and remodeled into a small country inn. None of the original
charm was lost. The rooms, though small, are neat, very
clean, and fully comfortable. The whole inn reflects
☛ Joan's tidy habits.

234

Food is hearty and homemade, prepared by the inn-keepers themselves. A great country breakfast is available daily.

After a day at the Marlboro Music Festival in the summer, or a day of skiing Mount Snow in the winter, it is nice to relax in the lounge that once was a carriage house. But music and skiing are not all. You have an 18-hole golf course at Mount Snow, tennis at hand, hiking, or just browsing. You also have a BYOB bar with piano, TV, and a fireplace.

How to get there: Wilmington is in southern Vermont. The inn is on Route 9, one mile west of the traffic light in town.

E: *I love old houses. This one is over 200 years old.*

The glowing carriage lamp beside the door
of a country inn when viewed through a cold rain
erases the rigors of the day
and promises a fine, fine evening.

On the Rocks Lodge
Wilmington, Vermont
05363

Innkeepers: Orla and Margie Larsen
Telephone: 802-464-8364
Rooms: 15, 13 with private bath.
Rates: $49.50 per person, double occupancy, MAP.
Facilities: Closed late October to early December, and April 15
    to mid-June. Breakfast, dinner, bar. Game room, li-
    brary, swimming pool, tennis courts, cross-country
    trails. Golf and downhill skiing nearby. No credit cards
    accepted.

If you decide to go hiking or skiing on any of the inn's
18 miles of cross-country trails, a good idea is to take Rockey,
the inn's Great Dane. If you get lost you need only say,
"Rockey, let's go home," and he will take you. Licke, a
Maine coon cat, is a beauty.

When you enter the living room you look out on the
heated pool and onto Mount Snow in the background.
Breathtaking! Off the dining room is a bright and cheery

bar where I had good fun with some inn guests when I was here last.

☛ Margie is the chef, and she turns out fine gourmet dining, some of the best in New England. All vegetables are fresh, and in summer the salads come from the inn garden. Orla meanwhile maintains an excellent wine cellar.

The rooms all overlook the gardens, and each has a view of the mountains. ☛ All are individually decorated with designer fabrics and wallpapers, in addition to color-coordinated towels and other great personal touches that make this inn very special.

The large couch in the living room is bright, flowered chintz, and nearby is a chess table. The whole room is a delight, with tremendous views any season of the year.

How to get there: From the only traffic light in Wilmington, go north on Route 100, 4.2 miles to a right fork in the road. Turn right and go approximately 1,000 feet over a bridge, and take your first right. Continue about 200 feet, turn left, and go up the hill. The inn is about one-quarter of a mile up, the first place on the left past the Trail's End Lodge.

E: *This is one inn I could move right into and stay, getting fatter and fatter as time passed. But what a way to go.*

The crackle of an inn's hearth
can melt the chilliest of minds and bodies.

Olive Metcalf

The Red Shutters Inn
Wilmington, Vermont
05363

Innkeepers: Loretta Klutsch and Charles Jones
Telephone: 802-464-3768
Rooms: Five, three with private bath, all with heat and smoke
   alarms.
Rates: $57, double occupancy, EP.
Facilities: Open all year. Breakfast, lunch in season, dinner,
   bar. TV in sitting room. No credit cards honored, but
   personal checks accepted.

The first time I saw the inn it was snowing, a beautiful
sight with the inn nestled upon a rolling hillside among the
pines, maples, and apple trees. The inn is a slate-roofed
Colonial. The grounds are well manicured and complete
with vegetable gardens and brook.

This is a chef-owned inn, and you know this usually
means good food. It certainly does here. Charlie has it all in
his head and cooks everything from scratch using ☞ the
best and freshest ingredients available. Some of the appetizers are Squid in Red Sauce with Linguine, and Frogs' Legs

in Garlic. The entrees are also intriguing; fresh, Poached King Salmon with a lemon dill sauce, or the chef's special, Garlic Shrimp, and duck, veal, steak, and on and on. Desserts, as you would expect, are glorious. Linzer Torte, long a favorite of mine, is just one of the many goodies.

Crackling fires in the dining room, sitting room, and cocktail lounge add to the charm of the inn, as does the summer porch with awning that is used for lunch.

The rooms are very comfortable and have private or semi-private baths. A touch of today I liked are the smoke and heat alarms they have.

Mount Snow is at hand for skiing, and nearby you have many lakes, tennis facilities, racquetball courts, and golf. The Marlboro Music Festival is right at hand, and the village itself can keep a good browser in ecstasy for hours.

How to get there: From I-91 at Brattleboro take Route 9 to Wilmington. The inn is at the west end of the village on the right.

❀

E: *The names of the animals at the inn are great: Puss Nips, the cat, and Raspberry Sundae, a very friendly Doberman.*

If I ever find an inn that bakes fresh macaroons daily,
I shall rent a room for a hundred years.

Olive Metcalf

The White House
Wilmington, Vermont
05363

Innkeeper: Robert Grinold
Telephone: 802-464-2135
Rooms: Eight, all with private bath, two with fireplace; one
    suite.
Rates: $45 to $85, per person. MAP.
Facilities: Closed April and May. Breakfast, dinner, Sunday
    brunch. Skiers' lunch in winter. Bar, swimming pool,
    cross-country skiing, health spa with sauna, whirlpool,
    steamroom. Credit cards accepted, but personal checks
    preferred.

The menu reads like one you would expect to find in
the White House, full of mouth-watering goodies served in
two dining rooms, both of which are ☛ very elegant. There
is also a small, private dining room.

Looking out one side of the inn you see rose gardens
with a fountain, and below this is a ☛ 60-foot swimming
pool. The grounds are well-groomed, and a pleasure to gaze
upon.

240

There are 18 miles of cross-country trails right here, which also make for wonderful walking in non-snow seasons. The inn has its own ski rental center, in addition to a large après-ski room open in the winter.

You have your choice of two bars. My favorite is on a large enclosed porch with hanging plants and skylights. The comfortable bar stools go well with the congenial bartender. Watching the snow fall on one of the skylights in the bar is very pretty.

The duck served here is beautifully presented. At the table the rib cage is lifted off and you have a nice ☞ boneless duck served with extra sauce that all ducks need.

As you walk through the gallery on the main floor you are looking at extremely ☞ unusual wallpaper that was printed in Paris in 1912. Add all of these things together, and you have a really good inn for year-round enjoyment.

How to get there: From Route I-91 take Route 9 to Wilmington. The inn is on your right just before you reach the town.

🍐

E: *Intrigue! Why did the original owner of the house put in* ☞ *a secret staircase? You will have to ask where it is.*

*The warmth of a country inn
can only be likened to
a well-made down comforter.*

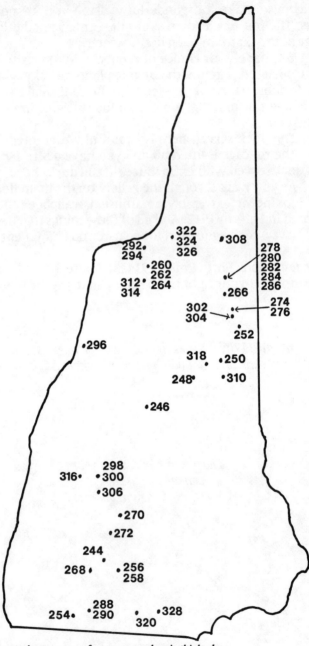

numbers on map refer to page numbers in this book

New Hampshire

olive Metcalf

David's
Bennington, New Hampshire
03442

Innkeeper: David Glynn
Telephone: 603-588-2458
Rooms: Two, each with private bath.
Rates: $40, double occupancy, EP.
Facilities: Closed Mondays, and December 1 to April 1. Breakfast for house guests only. Lunch, dinner, full license. No credit cards honored, but personal checks accepted.

I think David can feed about forty people, but he has overnight accommodations for only four. The rooms with their beamed ceilings and wide "illegal board" floors (so called because in those days boards over 12 inches in width were for the exclusive use of the King of England) are nice and cozy. The house belonged to David's grandmother, and he has fully restored it to its circa 1788 self. The walls had the original stencils by Moses Eaton, a famous man in his time. ☛ These designs have been duplicated throughout the whole inn.

Now for the best part, and that is David's food. His fame

stretches many miles in all directions. There were three of us enjoying his food, and, of course, I tried as much of it as I could. The Fresh Salmon Pie with an egg sauce was lighter than eating butterflies. The chicken and the lobster pies were sinfully delicious. The menu goes on, but I had to stop, well, not quite yet. We had one each of New England Deep-dish Apple Pie a la mode, Apricot Rum Cake a la mode, and David's Meringue Shell Vanilla Ice Cream with chocolate or strawberry sauce. I could hardly make it to the door. This is superb food. All breads and pastries are made here, and all of the vegetables are fresh.

There are jars of David's relishes, jams, and jellies for sale. Do take some home with you.

How to get there: Going north, exit from I-91 at Brattleboro and take Route 5 north to Route 9. Stay on 9 until North Branch, then turn right onto Route 31, which will take you into Bennington. David's Restaurant and Inn is across from the Town Hall in Bennington Square.

E: *The old carriage seat in the tiny sitting room intrigues me. From the surrey with the fringe on top?*

The Pasquaney Inn
Bridgewater, New Hampshire
03222

Innkeepers: Marge and Roy Zimmer
Telephone: 603-744-2712
Rooms: In summer, 28; in winter, 18; 10 with private bath.
Rates: $17 to $20, per person, double occupancy, EP; or $34 to $38, per person, double occupancy, MAP.
Facilities: Closed October 15 to Christmas. Breakfast, dinner, box lunches. Recreation barn, lawn games, lake swimming, boating, fishing, hiking, cross-country skiing. Golf, tennis, and downhill skiing nearby. MasterCard and Visa accepted.

The sideboard in the lobby of the inn is a 1790 Baltimore Hepplewhite, a thing of beauty. The living room, with a fireplace, looks out over Newfound Lake, as does the dining room. Dining at the inn is informal and relaxed, with all meals served family-style. ☞ Vegetables, always fresh, come from either the inn's ample gardens or the local markets. Best of all, the desserts and the breads are all done in the inn's own pastry kitchen.

Guest rooms are bright and attractive, some with a lake view, and the others with great views of the surrounding mountains. There are private and shared baths, and be sure to specify your wants when you make a reservation.

Basically Pasquaney is a family inn, with chidren always welcome. The recreation barn has a basketball court, shuffleboard courts, Ping-Pong, and a full, square dance floor with an old-fashioned caller's balcony. There is a calico cat called Mother Cat, and two other felines called simply Cat.

There is much to do here, no matter what season of the year. The inn has its own sandy beach on the lovely lake, also little skiffs for those who wish to take a row around the cove. Sailboats can be rented nearby. Golf and tennis are also near at hand. Winter brings skiing, spring means fishing for land-locked salmon or trout, and fall is that glorious foliage season. Newfound Lake is very reminiscent of the lake district of northern England, and beautiful.

How to get there: From I-93, take exit 23, turn left onto Route 104, then right onto Route 3A. The inn is on the right across from Newfound Lake.

🐟🐟

E: *The inn prepares box lunches for hikers, skiers and motor trippers. Nice touch.*

Corner House Inn
Center Sandwich, New Hampshire
03227

Innkeepers: Jane Kroeger and Don Brown
Telephone: 603-284-6219
Rooms: Four, one with private bath.
Rates: $22 to $30, single; $32 to $40, double occupancy; EPB.
Facilities: Open all year. Lunch and dinner. Skiing and hiking
  nearby. American Express and Visa accepted.

This is a very interesting town. Different. The inn is
centrally located so you can walk to everything. The
New Hampshire League of Arts and Crafts is here as well
as pottery shops, galleries, and museums. There are five
major ski areas within a short driving range.

The inn has been operating as an inn for over 100 years.
To keep pace with its history, the waitresses are in colorful
period pinafores. The food they serve is excellent. The
kitchen is famous for its ☞ crepes, and several different
ones are prepared each day. I have tried a few and, wow, are
they good. They also do fabulous things with soups. Another
great inn specialty is ☞ dessert; apple crisp or apple pie

stand out, and I dare you to eat just one of their cookies and not go back for more.

Of special note is the inn's house salad dressing. It is a buttermilk-dill combination. One of my party usually hates salad, but he ate it down to the last wisp of lettuce.

Roast duck is unusual. It is glazed with a variety of fruit sauces. And a new one on an old "inn creeper" like myself was Crab 'n Scallop Pie topped with puff pastry. Well, that tells enough about this good New Hampshire food.

The rooms are very comfortable. Bay windows in the living room, a spinning wheel, and plants give that touch of comfort you love in an inn. The carriage house is now the main dining room.

How to get there: Up I-93 to Exit 24, thence Route 3 to Route 113. Route 113 goes directly to Center Sandwich.

E: *Good inn animals are here. The cat is Anna and the dog, a golden retriever, is Cousteau.*

For one night at least
let me escape from all those things
the Puritans tell me I must face.
Let me find a friendly inn.

Stafford's in the Fields
Chocorua, New Hampshire
03817

Innkeepers: Ramona and Fred Stafford
Telephone: 603-323-7766
Rooms: 12, seven with private bath; cottages.
Rates: $55 to $75, per person, double occupancy, MAP.
Facilities: Open all year. Breakfast, dinner, Sunday brunch,
    liquor license. Trail lunches available. No smoking din-
    ing room. Parking. No pets. Clay tennis court, cross-
    country skiing. No credit cards accepted.

At the end of a quiet country lane sits a really lovely
country inn. It comes with a babbling brook, has forests at
hand, and overlooks some rolling fields. You will also find a
barn with truly unusual acoustics. ☛ Square dancing is fun
here in the summertime.

Ramona Stafford likes to cook in a sort of French
country style with wine and herbs and spices and, best of all,
with great imagination: Pork Tenderloin with Prunes, and
Stuffed Chicken Breast with almonds and raisins. The
daughter of the house, Mono, is responsible for the really

sinful desserts. Mother and daughter hold cooking classes. Oh, to live near them.

Breakfast is the way to start your day. Omelettes are different, sour cream with green chives, mild country cheddar, or cheddar and salsa. For Sunday brunch a real special is Eggs Hussard with Marchant du Vin. It translates to a wine merchant or a wine sauce in the vernacular. You could also try eggs Benedict or blueberry pancakes. You will not go wrong. Ramona serves well-balanced meals.

The inn is immensely comfortable with cross-country skiing right on the fields, and just utter peace. As Fred Stafford says there is an inexhaustible supply of "nature things to do." Just sitting, watching the swallows swoop or a leaf spin slowly to the ground restores what you may have lost in the hustle bustle of today's world.

Turn in the lane some snowy evening and see Stafford's glowing in the field, waiting to welcome you from a world well left behind.

How to get there: Take Route 16 north to Chocorua Village, then turn left onto Route 113 and travel one mile west to the inn. Or, from Route 93, take exit 23 and travel east on Route 104 to Route 35, and then to Route 16. Proceed north on Route 16 to Chocorua Village.

☀

E: *Bulah, a Brittany spaniel, lives here with a French Lop. A French Lop, to the uninitiated, is a beautiful black bunny.*

Darby Field Inn
Conway, New Hampshire
03818

Innkeepers: Marc and Marily Donaldson
Telephone: 603-447-2181
Rooms: 11, nine with private bath.
Rates: $40 to $60, per person, double occupancy, MAP.
Facilities: Closed in April and first three weeks in November.
Breakfast, dinner, bar. TV, library, swimming pool, ski-
ing, hiking. American Express, MasterCard, and Visa
accepted.

Set high atop Bald Hill in New Hampshire's White
Mountains with spectacular views of this wonderful country
is Darby Field Inn. Located 1,000 feet above Mount Washington Valley and only three miles from Conway Village, the inn
delights wanderers adventurous enough to leave the beaten
path.

The inn borders the ☛ White Mountain National
Forest where guests are welcome to cross-country ski, snow-
shoe, hike, or walk to nearby rivers, waterfalls, and lakes.

Rooms are charming, some with four-poster beds,

patchwork quilts, and braided rugs. Most rooms have private baths, and they are tucked away wherever space was available. How do you feel about an L-shaped shower stall?

Downstairs the inn's huge cobblestone fireplace is the center for warm conversation. If you want a bit livelier time come into the pub which sometimes features local singers.

Candlelight dinners begin with fine wine and a smashing sunset view up the valley. The food reflects the careful preparation of the chef. You'll always find a chef's special and fresh fish du jour. Whatever you order up here it will be excellent. Desserts are interesting. You must try Darby Cream Pie, quite different. The ☞ Irish Revolution will really end your day nicely.

Darby Field, a notorious Irishman, was the first white man to ascend Mount Washington. Had the inn been here in 1642, it is doubtful whether Mr. Field would ever have passed the pub.

How to get there: Turn on Bald Hill Road a half-mile south of the Kancamagus Highway on Route 16, then go one mile up the hill and turn right onto a dirt road. The inn is one mile beyond.

E: *The inn dogs are Malamutes, Akla and Chuska. Beautiful animals.*

> *A good innkeeper, a good cook,*
> *and an affable barkeeper*
> *are as standard in a country inn*
> *as a fire engine in a fire house.*

olive Metcalf

Fitzwilliam Inn
Fitzwilliam, New Hampshire
03447

Innkeepers: Charles and Barbara Wallace
Telephone: 603-585-9000
Rooms: 21, eight with private bath.
Rates: $22 to $26, single; $26 to $30, double; EP.
Facilities: Open all year. Breakfast, lunch, dinner, bar. TV,
   sauna, swimming pool, cross-country skiing. All major
   credit cards accepted.

"The more plastic motels that are built, the more people
are going to be driven back to a warm country inn, without
wall-to-wall carpeting, but with something else." Enoch
Fuller said this. And the Fitzwilliam Inn, which he owned
and operated until his death in 1973, is indeed a warm
country inn. The Fitzwilliam Inn is still the same old-
fashioned New England inn that has been offering food,
grog, and lodging to weary travelers since 1796.

If sleigh riding is your idea of a great winter sport, book
yourself in at Fitzwilliam. ☛ In summer there is square
dancing in the village, and there are also 12 antique shops in

this little town. The bar is a great little taproom, where hot winter drinks are called Broken Legs. Meals are hearty New England affairs, with a wonderful homemade pumpkin bread, and homemade desserts. All menus are tacked to little breadboards.

The Wallaces like to have music at the inn, so there are concerts on a regular basis year round. In summer you can enjoy the beautiful pool, after the sauna, and then lunch on the patio. All this, with the charm of a centuries-old inn, lovely antiques, and a cordial welcome from the innkeeper.

The men's room is a must. It has a blackboard for graffiti and a great red rocking chair for relaxing.

How to get there: The inn is 205 miles from New York, 65 miles from Boston. Vermont Transit buses stop at the door. It is on Route 119, just west of the intersection of Route 12.

E: *Over the fireplace hangs this word puzzle. The Wallaces will have to unscramble it for you.*

> *If the B mt put:*
> *If the B. putting:*
> *Don't put: over A - der*
> *You'd be an * it!*

Olive Metcalf

The Inn at Crotched Mountain
Francestown, New Hampshire
03043

Innkeepers: John and Rose Perry
Telephone: 603-588-6840
Rooms: 14, five with private bath, four with fireplace.
Rates: $30 to $45, double occupancy, EP.
Facilities: Closed first three weeks in November. Breakfast, dinner Tuesday through Saturday, bar. Tennis, swimming, cross-country skiing. Golf, fishing, and summer theater nearby. No credit cards accepted.

This 150-year-old Colonial house is located on the northern side of Crotched Mountain. There is a 40-mile view of the Piscataquog Valley, complete with spacious skies. Both innkeepers have gone to ☞ school to learn their trade, and what a charming house to practice it in. They are both pretty special themselves. Rose is from Singapore, and John is a Yankee.

Come and stay, there are many things to do. There are three golf courses in the nearby valley, fishing is great, and there is a wading pool for the young, as well as a 30 by

60-foot pool for real swimmers. Two areas provide skiing, one at the front door, and another down the road. Two clay tennis courts eliminate that tiresome waiting for a playing area. And come evening there are two summer theaters, one at Peterborough and another in Milford.

There are two English cockers who live here, Kong and Anan. Anan is Kong's daughter. There are numerous streams, ponds, and lakes for fishing and mountains for hiking. Golf is nearby. Come and enjoy this wonderful countryside with Kong and Anan. They would love to have you.

How to get there: Take 101A from Nashua to Milford, Route 13 to New Boston, and Route 136 to Francestown. Take Route 47 2½ miles, then turn left onto Mountain Road. The inn is one mile up the road.

E: *Any house that has nine fireplaces needs a wood lot and a man with a chain saw. Four of the bedrooms here have a fireplace, so remember to request one when you reserve.*

The register of a country inn
is a treasure of the names of good people.

The Inn at Tory Pines
Francestown, New Hampshire
03043

Innkeepers: Dick Tremblay and Jack Sullivan
Telephone: 603-588-6352
Rooms: 32, 28 with private bath; two suites; one cottage.
Rates: Rates start at $48.50, double occupancy, EP. Package
plans available.
Facilities: Open all year. Breakfast, lunch, dinner, bar. TV,
swimming, tennis, golf, golf pro shop, downhill and
cross-country skiing, skiing pro shop, ice-skating. All
major credit cards accepted.

The inn is the home of the ☛ Hall of Fame golf course,
which is patterned after the best 18 holes from famous
courses all over the world. Dick Tremblay is a PGA professional golfer. The inn has carts, lessons, clinics, and a good
practice range.

Skiing is also superb here. The inn is at the foot of
Crotched Mountain in the Monadnock region of southern
New Hampshire. There are excellent cross-country trails on
over 400 acres of the inn's own land plus ☛ guided moun-

tain tours for the more adventurous. Complete rental equipment is available, along with waxing and repair services.

The three dining rooms are extremely well furnished and comfortable. Two have fireplaces, and one of them has those great Indian shutters on the windows that fold back completely out of sight. The house is old, built in 1799. It is a Georgian Colonial. The bar has a 14-foot long pine top cut from one log, plus a fireplace. The lounge also has a huge fireplace. There is even a private dining room upstairs.

Food here is excellent. I had broiled scallops that the chef had made more than somewhat special, as he does with almost all of his dishes. The stuffed shrimp were huge. Eating my way through New England surely is fun, even if a bit fattening.

The rooms are across the road in what once was an old barn, but today you would never know it. All the rooms are super comfortable with great views. Two big maples, exactly as old as the house, flank the original entrance. They are called "wedding maples."

How to get there: From Hartford, take I-91 north to Brattle-boro, to Route 101 east to Peterborough. Then take Route 202 north to Bennington, New Hampshire and take Route 47. Tory Pines is 4 miles farther on the left. From Boston, take Route 3 to 101A west to Milford, New Hampshire, then a hard right at the rotary to Route 13 to New Boston, and Route 136 to Francestown. Bear right in the village. The inn is in 4 miles, on the right, on Route 47.

⧗

E: *On the pond where you skate live a gaggle of geese and two ducks.*

Olive Metcalf

Franconia Inn
Franconia, New Hampshire
03580

Innkeepers: Richard and Alec Morris
Telephone: 603-823-5542
Rooms: 29, 12 with private bath.
Rates: $45 to $49, per person, double occupancy, MAP. EP
rates also available.
Facilities: Closed mid-October to December 15, and April 1 to
May 25. Breakfast, dinner, bar, lounge. Swimming,
four tennis courts, horseback riding, Ping-Pong, hot
tub, skiing, soaring. All major credit cards accepted.

This is an inn in the fine tradition of old New England
hostelries. The rooms are simple and comfortable. Many of
the rooms connect with a bath, an ideal situation when you
bring youngsters, and this is an inn that welcomes children.
Never a dull moment any season of the year. While the
children play Ping-Pong or watch a movie, you can relax
in ☛ the lounge and listen to selected classical and popular
music by the glow of the fireplace.

A card room and a library are here for your enjoyment,

as is a screened porch overlooking the pool and the mountains. And they have something a bit unique, a game room for children, no adults alowed. Another entertainment for you is horseback riding. There are trail rides through Ham Branch stream and around the hay fields.

The living room is paneled with old oak and, with the fireplace, is very warm and cozy. The dining rooms, too, are gracious. There is a small one with a fireplace, a nice spot for breakfast. The food is very good, veal, rack of lamb, shrimp, steak, roast duck, chicken, all prepared with a gourmet touch.

There are 65 miles of cross-country trails right at hand, and they also have facilities so that you can ski from inn to inn on connecting trails. Downhill skiing is but ten miles away. Do come and enjoy.

How to get there: Take I-91 north to the Wells River-Woodsville Exit. Go right on Route 302 to Lisbon, New Hampshire. A few miles past Lisbon, go right on Route 117 to Franconia. Crossing the bridge into town, go right to the Exxon station. There, take another right to Route 116, and you're 2 miles to the inn. Or, if you have a single-engine plane, the inn has its own F.A.A.-listed airfield with a 3,000-foot long runway.

E: 🖙 *Horse-drawn sleigh rides in this beautiful winter wonderland are my idea of heaven.*

Olive Metcalf

The Horse and Hound
Wells Road
Franconia, New Hampshire
03580

Innkeepers: Sybil and Bob Carey
Telephone: 603-823-5501
Rooms: Seven, all with private bath.
Rates: $45 to $66, double occupancy, EP.
Facilities: Closed Wednesdays, and April and May. Dinner,
    Sunday brunch in summer, bar. Skiing, swimming. No
    credit cards accepted.

When you walk through the door of the inn you are
greeted by a small wooden hobby horse with a sign about its
neck that says, "No one over 11 will ride me." Children are
welcome at the inn only if well behaved and supervised at all
times.

The rooms here are bright, airy, and color-coordinated,
with nice views on all sides and ☞ fresh fruit to welcome
you.

Chamber music is played throughout the dinner hour.
Bob was in broadcasting and truly has an electronic closet

full of music. Dinner here is a gourmet's delight. The menu changes frequently, and dinners are prepared using house wines. For entrees there are treats such as Duckling with Apples, veal many different ways, Boeuf Bourguignon, interesting fish and vegetables. For starters, try a spinach crêpe with warm horseradish mayonnaise. I can taste it even now. All the baking is done at the inn.

There's an abundance of plants hanging and sitting in the picture window of the bar and lounge. You will also find a small but excellent library here.

How to get there: Take I-93 north, exit at Route 18, and turn left. The inn is on the left, several miles down the road.

♫

E: *One of the few funnies from Nixon's term is hanging on a wall near the ladies lounge. You must go and see it.*

*A good inn, good food, a warm bed and a loving woman
. . . heaven can be another time.*

Olive Metcalf

Lovett's by Lafayette Brook
Franconia, New Hampshire
03580

Innkeepers: Mr. and Mrs. Charles J. Lovett, Jr.
Telephone: 603-823-7761
Rooms: Seven in main house; cottages and dorm.
Rates: $38 to $54, per person, MAP.
Facilities: Closed after Columbus Day until after Christmas,
and April to July. Breakfast, dinner, bar. Swimming,
game room. Tennis, golf, riding, bicycling, fishing, and
skiing nearby. American Express, MasterCard, and Visa
accepted.

There are a lot of reasons for coming to The White
Mountains and Franconia Notch, and one of the best reasons
is this inn. It was constructed circa 1784, even before a road
was built through Franconia Notch. The inn is well into its
second generation of ☛ one-family ownership, and that
says a lot.

Charlie Lovett runs a fine inn. As he says, they work
hard at having the best table and best cellar in the North
Country. The menu changes daily. Some of the favorites are

lamb served with homemade chutney, veal and mush-rooms, eggplant with caviar, fresh shrimp mousse, and, at breakfast, sour cream cheddar cheese omelets, or shirred eggs with fresh mushrooms. These are but a few of the delights that Charlie comes up with. The inn has its own herb garden. At last count there were 37 different herbs at hand. No wonder the food is so good. Desserts, as you would expect, are heavenly.

There is a lovely terrace overlooking the mountains and the pool. Actually there are two pools. One is ☛ solar heated and the other fed from mountain springs. Oh, to be that hale and hearty for the latter.

A new addition to the area of Franconia Notch is the New England Ski Museum, an excellent review of a sport that goes back 5,000 years. It is important to preserve these rare artifacts.

How to get there: Take I-93 north, exit at Route 18 and turn left. The inn is on your right.

E: ☛ *The bar, the bar! From the staircase in a Newport Mansion, the marble bar is the most inviting spot I've run into in a month of Sundays.*

> *I never thought of business when awakened at an inn by the three o'clock chime of a nearby church.*

Bernerhof Inn
Glen, New Hampshire
03838

Innkeepers: Ted and Sharon Wroblewski
Telephone: 603-383-4414
Rooms: Nine, one with private bath.
Rates: $22.50 to $27.50, per person, EPB.
Facilities: Closed mid-November to mid-December, and mid-April to Memorial Day. Lunch July through October, dinner, bar. Sauna. All major credit cards accepted.

Fine European cuisine in the old-world tradition is what Ted and Sharon consider their outstanding food to be. Specialties include Wiener Schnitzel, Holstein Schnitzel, and even Schnitzel Cordon Bleu. Their desserts should be outlawed. Cherries Jubilee or Meringue Glacé are two of my fattening favorites, but delicious. They have an excellent wine list, and coffees for the gourmet finish.

Though some of the rooms are rather small, they are all clean, light, airy, and have good mattresses and box springs. These things I think are important to any inn.

The living room has a very unusual, tall, round coal

stove and a wonderful electronic machine. I hate electronics, but I make an exception for the "Piano Corder," an ingenious tape-playing gadget that plays the inn's Steinway. It is much more clever than the old pianos that played rolls.

The bar and lounge is called the "Zumstein Room," and it is a charming place, serving some really unusual food, like cheese fondues, Delice de Gruyère, Raclette, and always a quiche du jour.

You are but a few minutes from either North Conway or Jackson, so you will not lack for something to do absolutely any month of the year.

How to get there: From North Conway take Route 16 north. At Glen, turn left onto Route 302. The inn is on your right.

♡

E: *A free champagne breakfast in bed is yours on the third morning of your stay. It comes with eggs Benedict and fresh flowers. My, my.*

> *"The righteous minds of innkeepers*
> *Induce them now and then,*
> *To crack a bottle with a friend*
> *Or treat unmoneyed men."*
> —G. K. Chesterton

Olive Metcalf

The John Hancock Inn
Hancock, New Hampshire
03449

Innkeepers: Glynn and Pat Wells
Telephone: 603-525-3318
Rooms: Ten, all with private bath.
Rates: $45, double occupancy, EP.
Facilities: Closed one week in early spring, one week in late fall. Breakfast, lunch, dinner, lounge. Parking. Swimming, bicycles loaned. Skiing and tennis nearby. MasterCard and Visa accepted.

Operated as an inn since 1789, the John Hancock has nice, young owners, the Wells family. Carefully preserved is The Mural Room, believed to date back to the early years of the inn. The Carriage Lounge is very unusual, with tables made from giant bellows from an old foundry in Nova Scotia. Seats are made from old buggy seats. The name stems from the fact that John Hancock, the founding father, once owned most of the land that comprises the present town of Hancock. Set among twisting hills with a weathered clapboard facade, graceful white pillars, and a warm red door, the inn represents all that is good about old inns. Warm welcomes, good food, sound drinks, and good beds, set in a quiet town that hasn't changed much in the last two centuries.

Dinner is served by candlelight, and when winter storms howl through the hills the fireplace in the bar has a crackling fire to warm your heart and toes. Braided rugs cover part of the wide-board floors, and primitive paintings hang on the walls. There is a pastel of the inn, done in 1867, that the Wells were able to acquire.

Swim in summer in Norway Pond, within walking distance of the inn. Climb mountains, or just sit and listen to the church chimes during foliage time. Alpine and cross-country skiing are nearby in winter. Or browse in the antique shops on a cool spring morn.

How to get there: From Boston take Route 128, then Route 3 to 101 west. Hancock is located just off Route 202, 9 miles above Peterborough.

E: *The inn dog is a Lhasa named Nay-Daak Poo, which means "little innkeeper."*

We sat together round a single table and talked and heard each other in the quiet of the inn.

Olive Metcalf

Colby Hill Inn
Henniker, New Hampshire
03242

Innkeepers: The Glover Family
Telephone: 603-428-3281
Rooms: Ten, eight with private bath.
Rates: $38 to $45, single; $58 to $65, double; EPB.
Facilities: Open all year. Breakfast, dinner Tuesday through Sunday. Bar, TV, parking. Swimming pool. Skiing nearby. All major credit cards accepted.

This picturesque old house dates back to 1800. It leans and dips a bit here and there, but that only adds to the charm. The ☛ wide floorboards are authentic. You cannot find boards like that nowadays. Don Glover, Jr., is chief innkeeper. He supervises the cooking and everything else that needs doing in a country inn. While researching this book I have found innkeepers up in trees, down in cellars, chopping wood, and even doing dishes. Don can be found at any one of these activities.

Don's parents came up from New Jersey some years back to help Don run the inn. Don and his wife now have

270

four young Glovers, so they have moved out of the inn, taking Tar, the old welcoming inn dog, with them.

The meals are simple and delicious, with steak or chicken served many ways, fresh seafood, including salmon, and very good desserts, like lemon curd and chocolate mousse. The inn has its own garden, plus the use of the next door neighbor's garden, so in season there is a wealth of fresh vegetables.

Henniker is a small New England college town. Indeed, New England College is here. For skiers Pat's Peak, King Ridge, and Sunapee, which is also a state park, are close at hand. Cross-country trails abound in every direction, supplying every type of skiing and scenery.

How to get there: Go up I-91 to Brattleboro. Take Route 9 east into Henniker.

E: *The inn cat is Jelly Bean, and she has a few little beans around her.*

*With its swinging sign near
the hills it stands,
Vine-clad and filled with cheer.
'Tis a place to laze through
fresh, golden days
with sunlit peaks so near,*

*So good-bye to cares,
this spot is rare,
and we thank kind fate
for having brought us here.*

Stonebridge Inn
Hillsboro, New Hampshire
03244

Innkeepers: Nelson and Lynne Adame
Telephone: 603-464-3155
Rooms: Four, all with private bath.
Rates: $30, single; $35, double occupancy; continental breakfast included.
Facilities: Open all year. Closed Mondays and Christmas Day. Lunch, dinner, full license. Swimming and skiing nearby. MasterCard and Visa accepted.

These young innkeepers have a good bit of experience behind them, the best being that Nelson's father is the innkeeper of the New London Inn in New London, New Hampshire.

Nelson and Lynne have taken an old house and turned it into a small inn. There are four rooms, two large and two small, all with private bath.

Downstairs there are three dining rooms. One is done in wrought iron and glass, unusual and very pretty. The main dining room is a picture with ivory and chocolate napery dappled by flickering candlelight. There are a lot of windows in the inn, nice on a cloudy day.

The luncheon menu is interesting. From the kettle there are soups of all sorts, and the list on the sandwich board goes on forever. To accompany these good dishes you may select from four salads on their salad bowl list. Then from the cookstove come gems like quiche specials, chicken pot pie, and more.

Well, after all this luncheon choice, you know the dinner menu will be good. Just one example is Veal Gruyère, sliced veal, breaded and sauteed, then topped with sliced tomato, melted cheese, and shrimp. This is a different veal dish and a good one. There is, of course, much more, and the prices are moderate.

There is skiing nearby and summer swimming at Pierce Lake or Beard Brook. This is a very nice area. Do try it.

How to get there: From western New England take I-91 north to Exit 3 and then follow Route 9 east for a bit better than 40 miles. You will find the inn on your left as you enter town. From the Boston area take Exit 5 off I-89 and follow Route 9 west for 17 miles to Hillsboro.

E: *The inn's fried chicken is* *chicken with a New England difference. It is dipped into maple syrup batter before it is fried. Yum, yum!*

Olive Metcalf

Holiday Inn
Intervale, New Hampshire
03845

Innkeepers: Lois and Bob Gregory
Telephone: 603-356-9772
Rooms: Ten, all with private bath.
Rates: $35 to $42, per person, double occupancy, tax and
gratuity included, MAP.
Facilities: Closed late March to Memorial Day weekend, and
late October to December 26. Breakfast, dinner, BYOB.
Swimming pool, cross-country skiing. All major credit
cards accepted.

This Holiday Inn is a country inn, far removed from the
plastic cookie-cutter type of Holiday Inn you are accus-
tomed to. This is a modest country inn, good for families with
well-behaved children.

On the porch in winter, a wood-burning stove always
has 🐾 a kettle full of piping hot water on it, and the tea bags
are right at hand. There is also hot chocolate for skiers or just
plain cold people. For a drink you must bring your own
bottle, but the inn provides set-ups and ice. They also keep a

spot in their refrigerator if you wish to chill your own wine.

Displayed in the inn is Lois's ☛ collection of dolls; most are antiques and all are worth looking at.

The cottage next door was built for Marion Weston Cottle, the first female lawyer in New Hampshire. It is made of stone that looks as if it came from the nearby river bed, and it may have.

Dinner is served family-style, but usually with two entrees. Family-style dining is nice for a hearty appetite because you may have more than one helping, but, as Lois says, save room for the special desserts.

Cross-country skiing from the door on lighted trails at night is especially nice. The Holiday Inn and The New England Inn next door are both part of the Intervale Nordic Learning Center.

How to get there: North of North Conway take Route 16A off to your right. The inn is on your right.

E: *The solar heated pool is a nice modern addition.*

"There is nothing which has
been contrived by man by which
so much happiness is produced
as by a good tavern or inn."
—Samuel Johnson

The New England Inn
Intervale, New Hampshire
03845

Innkeepers: Linda and Joe Johnston
Telephone: 603-356-5541
Rooms: 26, 23 with private bath; ten suites with fireplace in village houses; four one-room cottages with fireplace.
Rates: $50 to $76, per person, double occupancy, MAP.
Facilities: Closed in April. Breakfast, dinner. Entertainment on weekends and holidays. Conference room, three clay tennis courts, swimming and wading pools, skating rink, cross-country skiing with lighted trails for night-time. American Express, MasterCard, and Visa accepted.

A landmark for travelers for nearly 190 years, The New England Inn started as a farm in the early 1800s. Today it is one of our really fine inns, chock-o-block with antiques and old pine paneling. The innkeepers will make you very comfortable. When you arrive at the inn, in any season, the sight is glorious, a white, rambling country inn in the shadows of the White Mountains.

The rooms are charming, clean and comfortable, and

after a full day, a pleasure to return to. The living rooms are gracious, plenty of chairs and couches, nice to curl up in with a good book, or, as I am prone to do, curl up with needlepoint.

☛ Anna Martins, the dining room named for a former owner, has superb food. Breakfast at Anna's starts with a juice and ☛ fresh fruit bar. They insist you try some of Stephanie's hot muffins and coffee cakes with lots of whipped butter. Dinner at Anna's is just what you would expect, expansive and delicious, ten different appetizers. One I just love is ☛ "Yesterday's Soup." Mom always did say it was better the next day. Maybe I am prejudiced but ☛ Chicken Elizabeth is grand. The inn's veal is famous among gourmets, only the finest is used. Do I like it here? You'd better believe it.

The Johnstons are involved with the Intervale Nordic Center. Between the inn and the Holiday Inn next door there are 35 kilometers of marked trails. Start off right by being outfitted in proper-fitting equipment, next take a lesson from a PSIA-certified instructor, and then go and enjoy cross-country skiing. The Intervale Tavern at the inn, with a blazing fireplace, serves skiers lunch and après-ski. A good hot chili is nice when you are cold.

How to get there: The inn is at the Gateway to the White Mountains, on Resort Loop, Route 16A, 3½ miles north of the village of North Conway.

E: *This good inn has good animals, Chessie the cat, and Brandy and Dickens the dogs.*

olive Metcalf

Christmas Farm Inn
Jackson, New Hampshire
03846

Innkeepers: Bill and Sydna Zeliff
Telephone: 603-383-4313
Rooms: 23, 14 in inn, nine with private bath; nine in 1771 saltbox, all with private bath. Six suites in sugarhouse and barn. One log cabin.
Rates: $42 to $52, per person, double occupancy, MAP. Special weekly and package rates.
Facilities: Open all year. Breakfast, dinner, pub. Swimming pool, game room, putting green, 80 kilometers of cross-country trails, golf, tennis, sauna, complimentary movies. Downhill skiing nearby. All major credit cards accepted.

Yes, Virginia, there is a Christmas Farm Inn, and they have the Mistletoe Pub and the Sugar Plum Dining Room to prove it. The food is fit for any Santa and his helpers, from the hearty, full country breakfast, which includes ☛ homemade doughnuts, muffins, and sticky buns, to gracious dinners that include three entrees each evening, two homemade soups, a full salad bar, homemade breads, and a complete dessert menu.

All of the rooms share Christmas names: Holly, Dasher, Prancer, Vixen, Donner, Cupid, Comet, and Blitzen.

Jackson is in the heart of the White Mountains, so bring your skis, or come in summer for the annual Christmas-in-July Week. ☛ There's a magnificent gala Christmas party Wednesday night with an outside buffet and Christmas tree, as well as live entertainment, dancing, shuffleboard, and golf tournaments. Santa must live nearby, because he never fails to arrive in a most unusual manner.

The inn dog is Freckles, and, of course, there is an inn cat, named Dynamite.

The food served here is excellent. The ☛ Medallions of Pork MacIntosh is glorious, and it also has a hint of brandy. Veal and chicken are so tender. Treats from the seas are real treats. The desserts do indeed make visions of sugarplums dance in your head, and all are made right here. How about apple pie, carrot cake, or the Christmas Farm special sundae? From here take a quick trip to the Mistletoe Pub for a nightcap.

Separate from the main building is the Christmas Farm function center. Perfect spot for not only medium to small business meetings, but also weddings, anniversaries, and the like. At one side of the room is a 12-foot wide fieldstone fireplace. There are also games of all sorts, a sauna, bar, and four nice suites.

How to get there: Go north on Route 16 from North Conway. A few miles after Route 302 branches off to your left you will see a covered bridge on your right. Take the bridge through the village and up the hill a quarter mile, and there is the inn.

E: *Making* ☛ *memories is something Bill and Sydna and their staff know all about.*

Dana Place Inn
3 Pinkham Notch Road
Jackson, New Hampshire
03846

Innkeepers: Betty and Malcolm Jennings
Telephone: 603-383-6822
Rooms: 14, seven with private bath.
Rates: $36 to $44, single; $28 to $34, double, per person;
EPB.
Facilities: Closed late October to mid-December, and mid-
April to mid-June. Dinner, piano bar. Parking. Cross-
country skiing, swimming, tennis, fishing. Downhill
skiing nearby. American Express, MasterCard, and Visa
accepted.

Located at the foot of Mount Washington, surrounded
by 600,000 acres of unspoiled National Forest, the Dana
Place Inn nestles in a beautiful valley next to the Ellis River.
The house was built in the mid-nineteenth century and
surely must have been a stagecoach stop. We know it was
once a farmhouse, set amid an apple orchard and built by
Antwin Dana. Set your own pace along lawns, gardens,

streams, meadows, and woodland trails. Walk through the orchard, past the swimming pool, take the country road past the tennis courts, along a mossy tree-shaded path, through a clearing, and ☛ there is a crystal-clear, rockbound pool in the Ellis River. Peace is beyond description.

Skiing is, of course, superb here, as well as hiking and mountain climbing for the experienced mountaineer. During school vacations lunch can be had at the inn, and in all seasons the kitchen specializes in picnic lunches. Come home to dinner and wonderful New England food, with more than a sophisticated continental touch. ☛ Choose between iced Gazpacho and Aunt Laura's Cold Peach Soup. In summer the vegetables come right out of Dana Place's own garden. Betty Jennings' dad has been chef at The New England Inn in Intervale for 30 years, so she knows about food and inns.

After a day of skiing, the place to unwind is the attractive bar. Enjoy hot buttered rum, hot mulled cider, good cheer, and if it is a weekend, the intimate piano music of Mike Jewell.

How to get there: Take I-95 north to Portsmouth, then the Spalding Turnpike to Route 16 north at Rochester. Follow Route 16 north past Jackson Village.

E: *The muppets are for sale, along with original watercolors by Myke Morton and David Baker.*

Olive Metcalf

The Inn at Thorn Hill
Jackson, New Hampshire
03846

Innkeepers: Donald and Gail Hechtle
Telephone: 603-383-4242
Rooms: 22, 16 with private bath.
Rates: $44 to $56, double occupancy, MAP.
Facilities: Closed April to mid-May, and November to mid-December. Breakfast, dinner, bar. Swimming pool, cross-country skiing. Downhill skiing nearby. No small children. All major credit cards accepted.

Mountains are everywhere you look from this inn. Relax on the porch in a ☞ New England rocking chair and enjoy the view. Even on a bad day it is spectacular.

There are two chefs who turn out scrumptious food. The chicken is ☞ boneless breast of chicken baked with spiced bread crumbs and laced with honey and bacon bits. The Lobster Pie is something special that is ordered by those who know how good it is. And their New England Clam Chowder is so good that it has been ordered as a dessert by some people.

The rooms are loaded with fine antiques. The beds are not only beauties, but they are comfortable as well. The wallpapers are very nice. The innkeepers are really working all of the time on the inn, and it surely does show it.

Winter brings skiing of all types. There are four alpine slopes in the area and 125 kilometers of good, groomed trails at all levels for cross-country skiing.

The Volvo International Tennis Tournament at the end of July is six miles away in North Conway. Also, Storyland is close by.

For skiers there is a shuttle bus service on weekends and holiday weeks that connects all Jackson inns to all of the slopes. The charge is nominal.

How to get there: Go north from Portsmouth, New Hampshire on the Spalding Turnpike (Route 16) all the way to Jackson, which is just above North Conway. At Jackson is a covered bridge on your right. Take the bridge, and just one block this side of the village center on the right is Thorn Hill Road, which you take up the hill. The inn is on your right.

E: *The living room, with a generous fireplace, has* 🖛 *a view that is unbelievable.*

> *And now once more I shape my way*
> *Thro' rain or shine, thro' thick or thin,*
> *Secure to meet, at close of day*
> *With kind reception, at an inn.*
> William Shenstone, 1714–1763
> (written at an Inn at Henley)

Olive Metcalf

Whitney's Village Inn
Jackson, New Hampshire
03846

Innkeepers: Terry & Judy Tannehill
Telephone: 603-383-6886
Rooms: 36, 30 with private bath; two cottages with fireplace.
Rates: $39 to $60, per person, MAP. Package rates available.
Facilities: Inn open all year. Dining room closed mid-April to
    mid-June, and late October to mid-December. Break-
    fast, dinner, bar. Hobo Lunch available. Library, game
    room. Skiing, ice-skating, tobogganing, tennis, swim-
    ming. American Express, MasterCard, and Visa
    accepted.

It's pretty nice to crawl out of bed, dress, have a sumptuous breakfast, and ☛ walk across to the lifts, trails, ski
shop or ski school, all just a snowball's throw away. Black
Mountain is right here. The lifts can handle 2,900 skiers per
hour, so there is hardly any waiting. Fifteen trails serve the
mountain, and all are kept in the best condition possible.

A lighted skating rink is right beside the inn. Bring your
own skates, or rent them here. The inn also has tobogganing,

a sport everyone should try at least once.

The dining room is truly a garden spot, with plants hanging all about, herbs growing in a large cart to be used by the chef, flower flats on each table for holding salt, pepper, sugar, and a copy of Burpee's Farm Annual. Old Burpee posters are on the walls. Another flower cart holds the salad, another the vegetables, and a fourth the desserts. It's very impressive to look beyond all this and see the skiers arriving at the base of the mountain.

Tea is served at 4:00 every afternoon in the living room. This, too, is where you have your before and after dinner drinks.

The Shovel Handle Lounge is a most unique pub in a beautifully restored barn adjacent to the inn. This barn offers panoramic views of Black Mountain. After skiing, and after dinner, enjoy your favorite beverage served up in pint Mason jars. Very different. And do join the Pub Mug Club. Bring in your own mug, receive a card and a tee shirt, and then your mug hangs here for your exclusive use. There is a television in the pub for special events, a huge fireplace, and great fun. If you are hungry, the pub's own kitchen can serve you some chili. Or you can read a book, for there is a good library here. There is just no end to the things you can do.

How to get there: Go north from Conway 22 miles on Route 16. Take a right on Route 16A through a covered bridge, into Jackson Village. Take Route 16B to top of hill to the inn.

E: *I love the Hobo Lunch, served continental or American-style in a small burlap bag, plus your choice of either French wine or imported natural fruit juices.*

285

olive Metcalf

The Wildcat Inn
Jackson, New Hampshire
03846

Innkeepers: Pam and Marty Sweeney
Telephone: 603-383-4245
Rooms: 18, eight with private bath.
Rates: $21 to $28, EPB.
Facilities: Closed May and November. Breakfast, lunch, dinner, bar. Sunday brunch in summer. Music in lounge. Downhill and cross-country skiing, hiking. American Express, MasterCard, and Visa accepted.

The big old front porch has been converted into a dining room. It is sad to lose a porch, but this is such a popular spot the space was needed. Take a look at the menu and you will see why they needed more dining space; all their food is ☛ interestingly different, and so good. The ☛ pie crust is the best I ever had, and the fillings they put in them are delicious. All of the desserts are lovingly made by Pam. There are good soups, fine quiches, and chili with a hearty tang. Not just the same old cuisine, the food here will titillate your taste buds.

The Wildcat is a real old-time country inn, but there is nothing old-fashioned about the food or entertainment. In the big, old Tavern with two large fireplaces, you will find live musical entertainment, maybe a flautist, a lutanist, or a classical guitarist. Whatever it may be, you can count on it being good.

The inn is right next to both alpine and cross-country skiing. One-hundred-and-twenty-five kilometers of maintained, well-groomed trails start at the front door, near the touring headquarters, and end in the backyard beside the heated waxing hut. You can get touring skis, boots, alpine ski equipment, and touring instructions just a few strides from the inn's front door. And when the snows melt, you will find these trails glorious for walking or hiking. Jackson is a good spot anytime of year.

How to get there: Take Route 16 north from North Conway. Take Route 16A to your right, through a covered bridge, and into Jackson. The inn is in the center of town.

E: Five downhill ski areas, with established ski schools only a few minutes away, are pretty nice; so are the inn dogs, Sassafras and Paco.

olive Metcalf

Woodbound Inn
Jaffrey, New Hampshire
03452

Innkeeper: Jed Brummer
Telephone: 603-532-8341
Rooms: 33, 31 with private bath; 13 cottage units.
Rates: $50 to $60, per person, double occupancy, AP.
Facilities: Open all year. Breakfast, lunch, dinner. Play barn,
ski school and rentals, swimming, golfing, tennis, boat-
ing, fishing. Major ski areas nearby. American Express,
MasterCard, and Visa accepted.

Woodbound is perfect for families, and caters rather
well also to us older folks. It has been a vacation resort since
1892. This is a self-contained country resort on the shores of
Lake Contoocook, and, as the brochure says, has over 200
acres of woodland, sandy beaches, and great hiking and
walking trails. Swimming, sailing, canoeing, boating, fishing,
a par three, 1,200-yard nine-hole golf course, a putting
green, tennis, volleyball, croquet, horseshoes, and shuffleboard, are all available on the premises. And inside the Play
Barn you'll find Ping-Pong, pool, shuffleboard, electronic

games, and an intriguing music machine. The whole complex has a relaxed, informal, homey atmosphere.

The inn provides real home-cooked meals, and when the weather is right, great cookouts. All breads and pastries are homemade. The fresh vegetables and salad makings come from the inn's nearby gardens.

The cottages, each with its own fireplace or Franklin stove, vary in size accommodating two to eight people. Very attractive.

Children are well taken care of with supervised programs and activities. There is a baby-sitting service available night or day.

The Brummer family, all of them, run the inn, and all you have to do is ask and you will be taken care of speedily and nicely.

How to get there: From New York follow I-91 to Bernardston, Massachusetts. Proceed on Route 10 to Winchester, then take Route 119 to Rindge and watch for signs to the inn. From Boston follow Route 2, then Route 119 to Rindge.

E: *I just love a real family country inn.*

. olive Metcalf

The Monadnock Inn
Jaffrey Center, New Hampshire
03454

Innkeeper: Sally Roberts
Telephone: 603-532-7001
Rooms: 14, seven with private bath.
Rates: $30 to $40, double occupancy, continental breakfast
   included.
Facilities: Open all year. Dining room closed on Mondays,
   Christmas Eve, and Christmas Day. Lunch Tuesday
   through Friday, dinner Tuesday through Saturday,
   Sunday brunch, bar. Cross-country skiing. MasterCard
   and Visa accepted.

Three sets of innkeepers have operated this inn since
1920. Sally Roberts has been the innkeeper for several years,
and what a terrific job she is doing. The house has been here
a long time, and I hope she will be here lots longer.
   From the minute you set foot on the wide front porch
until you sink into your comfortable four-poster at night you
will be happy at this lovely inn. There is so much to do. Have
you ever been to the Cathedral in the Pines? It's not far. Have

you ever wanted to get really involved in maple sugaring? This is the place. It can be arranged with a snap of the fingers.

Sally likes to think the Monadnock Inn is capable of taking you back in time. But it was never this good. The food is worth writing home about. The cheesecake, by their own admission, is inn-famous. Baked Oysters with parmesan cheese is just one appetizer. Sauted Pork Tenderloin in mustard sauce or Roast Cornish Hen in devilled sauce are but two of the entrees. This is different food, and very good.

In brisk winter weather there is always a roaring fire in one of the fireplaces and miles of cross-country trails for skiers. Or come in the fall for wonderful, glorious foliage. Autumn in New Hampshire should have a song all its own.

How to get there: The inn is located on Route 124, southeast of Keene, a scant 2 hours from Boston.

E: *There aren't many places like this around. Cherish it.*

> *I was lost, I was tired, I was discouraged,*
> *and then I found a friendly inn.*

Beal House Inn
Littleton, New Hampshire
03561

Innkeepers: Doug and Brenda Clickenger
Telephone: 603-444-2661
Rooms: 14, 9 with private bath.
Rates: $25 to $45, double occupancy, EP.
Facilities: Open all year. Breakfast. Dinner for groups by
   arrangement and on holidays. Antique shop. All major
   credit cards accepted.

The Beal House was built in 1833 as a farmhouse and
barn. Like most farms in New England, over the years the
house and barn became connected into one continuous
building. Ultimately it all became converted into an inn. The
inn has an antique shop, but is also an antique shop in itself,
for all the furnishings are for sale. You can 🖝 sleep in a bed
you may wind up buying. This is a good way to go antiquing;
try before you buy.

   All the rooms are clean and neat. The front rooms
have 🖝 glorious four-poster beds. There also is an upstairs
sitting room, small but cozy.

Breakfast is bountiful. Doug is the chef, and his specialty is popovers. Of course he does all sorts of other good things. His dining room has a fireplace, and is set with beautiful blue willow plates. Off of this room is the porch, full of wicker furniture and potted plants. Menus of all nearby restaurants are at hand for your perusal.

This is a lovely area to visit, not far from Franconia Notch and the Old Man of the Mountain. You also have Crawford Notch nearby. Do take a drive down the notch and look at the railroad they pinned to its west side. When you see it you cannot believe it.

The inn is in town so that you have the whole town of Littleton to walk about and see.

How to get there: From I-93 take Exit 42, turn right, and go one mile to the intersection of Route 18 and Route 302. This is Main Street and the inn is here.

━O

E: *The gazebo in the back yard is charming.*

A good innkeeper, a good cook,
and an affable barkeeper
are as standard in a country inn
as a fire engine in a fire house.

Edencroft Manor
Littleton, New Hampshire
03561

Innkeepers: Laurie and William Walsh, Jr.,
   Barry and Ellie Bliss
Telephone: 603-444-6776
Rooms: Six, four with private bath.
Rates: $20 to $40, double occupancy, EP.
Facilities: Closed first two weeks in March. Restaurant closed
   Mondays. Breakfast for house guests, lunch Tuesday
   through Saturday every season but winter. Dinner.
   Cross-country skiing, snowmobiling. American Ex-
   press, MasterCard, and Visa accepted.

The grand, old Victrola (and it works) sitting in the
living room took me back to my childhood with nice memories of winding ours up and listening to the records. The inn
has a huge collection of them. A large fireplace and plenty of
books are also in this room. All in all, very charming. For
your garden buffs there is a small solarium with plants and
antiques just off this room.
   The bedrooms have color names. The brown room has

its own fireplace. The gold room is yummy with two double beds at angles to each other. Also, this is a bright, cheery room. In all the rooms are homemade quilts. One is done with old neckties and is just grand.

Sitting in the lounge-bar area you are overlooking both Cannon and Lafayette Mountains. Beautiful in winter, and equally beautiful any other season with the hanging plants overhead.

All breads, desserts, and soups are made right here. A special of theirs in a "Melt." This is an open-faced sandwich with lettuce, tomato, and melted cheese plus a wide range of ingredients you can add as you wish, tuna, ham, turkey, roast beef, or a special vegetarian mix. How about a combination? This menu is very inventive and good food results.

How to get there: Take I-93 to its very end just above Littleton, New Hampshire. Turn left on Route 18. Go halfway up the hill and turn right onto Route 135 north. Three-tenths of a mile further on, on your right, is the inn.

E: Six appetizers, four soups and a lovely dessert cart . . . too much.

Lyme Inn
Lyme, New Hampshire
03768

Innkeepers: Fred and Judy Siemons
Telephone: 603-795-2222
Rooms: 15, ten with private bath.
Rates: $50 to $65, double occupancy, EPB.
Facilities: Closed three weeks after Thanksgiving and two weeks in late spring. Dining room closed Tuesdays. Dinner, bar. Near Dartmouth College, golf course, canoeing, fishing, and skiing. No children under eight. All major credit cards accepted.

This lovely inn sits at the end of the common of this quiet New Hampshire town. The inn dates back to 1809. All of the original rooms have been restored in keeping with the age of the building, and each bedroom is filled with  antiques and its own unique character.

The tavern has a neat, small fireplace with glary cat-eyed andirons. Here on a cold night a cheese fondue is a must. Next door in the dining room do not miss the fresh spinach salad served with bacon bits and chopped egg. The house dressing is, to quote me, ☞ fantastic. But then, so is everything else from breakfast through dinner. TheWiener Schnitzel is very light, delicious. Their use of garlic is liberal and delightful. The chef really does credit to his kitchen.

There is an extensive library for guests to enjoy. You are ☞ encouraged to take home a partially read book and return it when you are finished. This is nice.

There is much to do in the area. Great walking, great hiking, and wonderful skiing. But a few miles away is Dartmouth College with its Ivy League sports competition and fine cultural events. Locally you have a golf course, and there is canoeing on the Connecticut River. There are many secluded ponds for the fisherman to try his luck. And of course you have antique shops all about.

And do try a hot dog at the general store just on the other side of the common. Rare treat.

How to get there: Take Exit 14 from I-91. The inn is located east of the interstate on Route 10 right at the village common.

ᑐ

E: *The wicker furniture on the huge screened porch is enchanting.*

> *A glass of good whiskey*
> *before an open fire in a good inn*
> *is an unspoken toast to life*
> *as it should be lived.*

olive Metcalf

Hide-Away Lodge
New London, New Hampshire
03257

Innkeepers: Lilli and Wolf Heinberg
Telephone: 603-526-4861
Rooms: Eight, all with private bath.
Rates: $26 daily, $170 weekly, EP. MAP rates available.
Facilities: Closed Tuesdays and November to mid-May. Dinner, bar. Little Lake Sunapee, golf, tennis, and summer theater nearby. No credit cards accepted.

When I drove into this lovely old house and met the host, Wolf Heinberg, who has a most engaging smile, I knew I had found something special. Already I had heard about the food served here, and after talking with Wolf I was sure all I had heard was true. Thankfully I was able to stay in the last room available in the inn.

Dinner hour arrived, and I went down to the cocktail lounge, The Pipedreaming Pub. I placed a cocktail order, drooled over the menu, ordered dinner, and asked for the wine list. Wolf suggested that maybe a look in the wine cellar would help me decide. I followed him into a ☞ huge, temperature-controlled wine cellar. Fantastic, every wall was covered with wine. In the center of the room is a large table with silver candelabras and a beautiful wine book. Wolf is a very proud man, and he should be. The inn carries four stars in the Mobil Guide.

☛ The inn will, on 24-hour notice, and for any number of people, prepare a gourmet feast. Included are pheasant, rack of lamb, venison, and many others. The regular menu is a dream. Crisp duckling with peach glaze is a favorite, not to mention many veal delights, fresh vegetables, and desserts about which I could write a whole chapter. As if this were not enough, there are bits of poetry all over the inn written by Wolf. You must come and read them. But call ahead, reservations are a must.

How to get there: Follow Main Street in New London past Colby-Sawyer College to the blinker light at the north end of town. Go straight ahead and follow the signs to the inn about 2 miles from town.

⏳

E: *I wanted to stay in the wine cellar.*

olive Metcalf

New London Inn
New London, New Hampshire
03257

Innkeepers: George and Clara Adame
Telephone: 603-526-2791
Rooms: 26, all with private bath.
Rates: $25 to $35, single; $30 to $40, double; EP.
Facilities: Open all year. Breakfast, lunch, dinner. Breakfast
    the only meal served on Christmas Day. Nelson's
    Tavern. Parking. Skiing, two public beaches nearby.
    MasterCard and Visa.

This inn, which has been serving the traveler since
1792, is blooming anew under the direction of the Adames.
    The old inn is full of beautiful antiques. It's worth a trip
to stop and look and eat, even if you can't stay.
    New London is the home of Colby-Sawyer College.
There is always something going on at the college. Also, the
New London Barn Players is the oldest summer theater in
New Hampshire.
    The rooms are nice, large, comfortable, most of them
with cross-ventilation and louvered doors. Nelson's Tavern

is a good spot for a quick, light meal. Love the old trunks used as cocktail tables. The dining room is very gracious, serving good food such as sauteed Veal du Chef, scallopini with fresh mushrooms and shallots flamed in vermouth with veal stock and heavy cream. Honey Almond Pheasant is another winner. All breads and pastries are baked right here.

In the summer guests have beach privileges at Little Lake Sunapee.

This is a beautiful part of the world any time of year, so come on up.

How to get there: Take Exit 8 at Ascutney, Vermont from I-91. Follow signs to Claremont, New Hampshire. Take Route 11 east to Newport, Sunapee, Georges Mills, and New London. There is bus service via Vermont Transit from Boston, and from White River Junction, Vermont.

E: *New London is a lovely town. Do come up and enjoy it.*

When the stars are lost and rain seeps coldly upon the ground, how wonderful to find a lighted inn.

olive Metcalf

The Scottish Lion
North Conway, New Hampshire
03860

Innkeepers: John and Phyllis Morris; owners, Jack and Judy
   Hurley.
Telephone: 603-356-6381
Rooms: Eight, five baths.
Rates: $20 per person, EPB.
Facilities: Open all year. Closed Christmas Eve and Christmas
   Day. Lunch, dinner, bar. Parking. Import Shop, free
   catalogue available. All major credit cards accepted.

The rooms are cozy, one has an eyelet-trimmed canopy
bed, another a spool bed with a patchwork quilt. All are
charming. A hearty Scottish breakfast is served to house
guests. The whole inn is full of fine 🖝 Scottish paintings. Do
not miss any of them.

Food, of course, features the best of Scottish touches
and is rated three stars in the Mobil Guide. Highland Game
Pie which is venison, beef, hare, and fowl simmered in wine
and baked in puff pastry may sound strange, but a gentleman
spoke to me who had had it the night before. His report,

"Delicious." Hot Scottish oatcakes are served instead of bread or rolls. A marvelous dish named Rumbledethumps is one of the potato choices, what a taste. I must tell you one more; Forth Lobster Lady Tweedsmuir, tender pieces of lobster in a delicate cream and Drambuie sauce, stuffed in the shell. You must try this dish.

The inn has a long list of special pleasures from the pub such as a Hoot Mon cocktail, St. Andrews Hole-in-One or Loch Ness Monster, and more and more. For dessert, Scottish Trifle or Scots Crumpets with fresh fruit and honey are but a few. The inn also serves a very special coffee.

The Import Shop features the finest of imports from Scotland, England, and Ireland. They have over ☞ 300 different tartan ties, plus wools, cashmeres, crystal, thistle pottery, and much more. Do go and enjoy.

How to get there: Take Route 16 to North Conway. The inn is one mile north from the center of town, on the left.

E: *When you come down the road and see the magnificent flag streaming out in the wind you just can't go by. Stop for a drink, if you can't stay the night. You'll love it.*

olive Metcalf

Stonehurst Manor
North Conway, New Hampshire
03860

Innkeeper: Peter Rattay
Telephone: 603-356-3113
Rooms: 26, 23 with private bath; two suites.
Rates: $42 to $92, double occupancy, EP. MAP rates available
in summer and fall.
Facilities: Open all year. Breakfast, dinner, bar. Meeting room
for up to 50 people. Pool, tennis, shuffleboard, volley-
ball. All major credit cards accepted.

This turn-of-the-century mansion is a fine country inn.
Set back from the highway among stately pine trees, it makes
you think you are going back in time, and in a way you are.
The front door is huge. Once inside, you see beautiful
oak wood and wonderful wall-to-wall carpet. The room to
the left is all wicker and all comfort. Ahead of you is the
warm living room, with walls full of ☛ books, and a huge
fireplace. The unusual screen and andirons were made in
England. To the right of the fireplace is a 12-foot, curved
window seat of another era. The lounge area has a ☛ two-

seat bar, just the right size.

Relax in a high-back wicker chair in the dining room and enjoy the fine, gourmet delights of steaks, seafood, chicken, or one of the ☞ six different veal dishes served here. Desserts are just spectacular.

The staircase is a beauty, and the large rooms are beautifully appointed. ☞ Fantastic wallpapers and beautiful carpets all add to this great inn. The third floor rooms have windows at odd angles, dictated by the roof line of the house. Some rooms have porches, and one has a stained-glass door going out to its porch. There is a lot of lovely stained glass throughout the inn.

Their pool is the largest in the Mount Washington area, and is made of ☞ wood, the only wooden one I have ever seen. You swell it in the spring, just as you would a wooden boat. Cocktails are served around the pool in the summer. There are tennis courts, shuffleboard and volleyball courts. Plenty of things will keep you busy, or, like me, you might want to just sit and relax.

How to get there: The inn is on Route 16 just a short distance north of North Conway.

E: *On the second floor, in one of the hall bathrooms, is a wood-enclosed steel bath tub. Quite a sight.*

olive Metcalf

Follansbee Inn
North Sutton, New Hampshire
03260

Innkeepers: Larry and Joan Wadman
Telephone: 603-927-4221
Rooms: 23, 11 with private bath.
Rates: $25 to $38, double occupancy, EP.
Facilities: Inn closed two weeks in April and two weeks in
    November. Restaurant closed Mondays. Breakfast,
    dinner, lounge. Cross-country skiing from the inn,
    swimming, boating. Downhill skiing and golf nearby.
    MasterCard and Visa accepted.

North Sutton has an old church with an old clock that
chimes out the time. What a wonderful sound to hear. Next
door is Follansbee, and you smell great things when you
enter this fine inn.

The food at the inn is superb. ☞ All soups, breads,
salad dressings, and desserts are made right here. ☞ The
potato is baked and stuffed, and it's a pleasure to get one
piping hot. There are several steaks to choose from, and
hand-breaded onion rings taste as divine as they sound. You

could try the trout, or scampi, either crab or shrimp. Add to these, veal, prepared three different ways, chicken, and linguini. But you haven't had it all until you try the home-made desserts. The dining room you are in has comfortable captain's chairs and touches of chintz and crisp linen. A lovely setting for the superb food.

There is much to do in the area, such as riding, golf, skiing, or just sitting in the living rooms with a book or needlework. The rooms are amply bright and comfortable. What more could one want? This is a lovely inn.

How to get there: Take I-91 north to Ascutney, Vermont. Follow Route 103 to Route 11 east, to Route 114. Proceed to North Sutton. The inn is behind the church.

E: *The innkeepers have traveled all over the world, and the inn reflects the treasures they accumulated.*

A night at an inn adds a tinge to the coming day that cannot be described, only be enjoyed.

Philbrook Farm Inn
Shelburne, New Hampshire
03581

Innkeepers: Connie Leger and Nancy Philbrook
Telephone: 603-466-3831
Rooms: 19, six with private bath; five cottages with house-keeping arrangements.
Rates: $30 to $35, per person, double occupancy, MAP. Cottage $200 weekly.
Facilities: Closed April and late October to December 26. Breakfast, lunch, dinner ,BYOB lounge. Library, pool table, Ping-Pong, cross-country skiing, snowshoeing, hiking. Downhill skiing nearby. No credit cards accepted.

In 1861 Philbrook Farm started as an inn. Today it is still an inn and still has Philbrooks living here, running it in fine New England tradition. With over 1,000 acres there is plenty of room to roam any season of the year.

This is a very peaceful and relaxed inn. ☛ The library is comfortably crowded with good books. Fireplaces are all over. There is even a player piano in the dining room. A lovely Victorian living room has card tables and an old pump organ. The TV lounge has walls of Currier & Ives prints plus a good fireplace.

Food is served here family-style and prepared from scratch. The baked goods are made daily. Every Sunday features roast chicken, and Sunday morning fare is pure New England, with codfish balls and corn bread. Saturday gives another New England special, namely baked beans. The gardens provide fresh vegetables and good salads, and the homemade soups are a meal in themselves.

Bedrooms are furnished with antiques, some lovely, four-poster beds, and a collection of old bowl and pitcher sets, really the best I have ever seen.

How to get there: The inn is 1½ miles off Route 2. Going west, look for a direction sign on your right, and turn right. Cross the railroad tracks and then a bridge. Turn right at the cross-roads and go a half-mile to the inn, which is on North Road.

E: *The playroom, with its collection of* 🐾 *old farm tools and kitchen utensils, is a nice reminder that sometimes nice things are saved.*

You cannot hide a good country inn.

Snowvillage Lodge
Snowville, New Hampshire
03849

Innkeepers: Pat and Ginger Blymer
Telephone: 603-447-2818
Rooms: 14, all with private bath.
Rates: $65 single; $47.50 per person, double occupancy; MAP. Special package rates available.
Facilities: Open all year. Breakfast, dinner, bar, lounge. Cross-country skiing, ski rental and instructions, tennis. Downhill skiing, racquetball, hiking, canoeing, and riding nearby. All major credit cards accepted.

Hollywood has lost a good lighting director and an award-winning hairdresser for the stars, but Snowvillage has won a set of better-than-average innkeepers. Pat has become a very good chef, doing everything just right. I had the best ☛ Veal Picatta ever here.

There is one main course served each night, and whatever it might be, rest assured it will be scrumptious.

The view from the inn is breathtaking. Mount Washington and the whole Presidential Range, plus the rest of the White Mountains, greet your eyes everywhere you look. In summer at the top of Foss Mountain, right at the inn, you can eat your fill of wild blueberries.

Rooms are comfortable and spacious, with tons of ☛ towels in luscious colors. The living room, with a huge fireplace and comfortable couches all around, makes this an inn to relax in. A huge porch surrounds the inn. Sit out here and enjoy the view.

There is a service bar and lounge, and here you can meet the four-footed members of the family. The dogs are Flump and Louise. Three cats come in four colors. Hound Dog is the gray beauty, BN (for black nose) is black and white, and Hannibal is orange all over.

For you inveterate shoppers, fear not; North Conway is but 15 or 20 minutes away.

Ginger is everywhere you need her, and ☛ just is a natural innkeeper.

How to get there: Out of Conway on Route 153, go 5 miles to Crystal Village. Turn left, go about 1½ miles, turn right at the Snowvillage sign and go up the hill, ¾-mile to the inn.

E: *Plants are everywhere. I have a slip from a huge cactus.*

Olive Metcalf

The Homestead
Sugar Hill, New Hampshire
03585

Innkeepers: Esther Serafini and Barbara Serafini Hayward
Telephone: 603-823-5564, 603-823-9577
Rooms: 17, 10 in main house, all with running water; 7, all
    with private bath, across the street.
Rates: $40 to $48, per person, MAP.
Facilities: Closed mid-March to Memorial Day, and Novem-
    ber 1 to December 24, except for Thanksgiving week.
    Breakfast, dinner. Jacket requested for dinner. BYOB.
    No credit cards accepted.

Essie Serafini is a legend in her own time. She has been
at the inn for 60 years. Her first job, at the age of 10, was to
pass the relish tray. The inn recently celebrated 100
years, and good friends presented Essie with a magnificent
$8,000 Gulbransen electric organ. Essie does not read music
and does not have to. Wow, can she play. Back 100 years her
family charged $3.00 a week for room and board.

There are many original family antiques which furnish
the rooms of The Homestead. One of the beds, a pine four-

poster, came by ox cart from Richmond, New Hampshire. In the parlor is a hand-hooked rug, 9 feet by 5 feet, all about New Hampshire that identifies dozens of landmarks, animals and birds. This rug was done by Essie. She also wrote a delightful booklet titled, "Tales, Tours and Taste Treats," full of folklore, on sale at the inn or next door at the Sampler, a shop run by Essie's daughter, Barbara.

The rooms are spotless, what else would you expect from this lady, and the food is superb. Essie still finds time to do most of this. She is a powerhouse of a woman.

The inn has a very special thing about Thanksgiving week. People come from all over for this special treat, but reserve early

How to get there: Take Exit 38 from I-93 to Route 117. The Homestead is about 3 miles up the hill on Route 117. Or coming from the west, turn east on Route 117 from Route 302.

E: *Essie is such a special, warm, wonderful person, I just love her.*

Sunset Hill House
Sugar Hill, New Hampshire
03585

Innkeepers: Betty Lou Carmichel and Douglas Reed
Telephone: 603-823-5522
Rooms: 35, 33 with private bath.
Rates: $60 to $65, single; $45 to $47.50, per person, double occupancy; MAP.
Facilities: Open all year. Breakfast, lunch, dinner, bar, lounge. Nine-hole golf course, putting green, croquet, swimming pool, shuffleboard, cross-country ski shop, touring trails, beauty shop, gift shop. American Express, MasterCard, and Visa accepted.

The view from the inn is spectacular. You are seeing the Presidential and Franconia ranges of the White Mountains, and, as the innkeepers say, they are above the fog-line.

You can see from the list under "facilities" that there is something for everyone to do here. ☛ Children are more than welcome, (well-behaved ones, of course).

There are five dining rooms, all very nicely done, along the back of the inn with incredible views of the White

Mountains and the pool. The pool, by the way, is really unique, having a separate ☛ whirlpool section with a waterfall down to the regular pool. Very nicely done. The inn serves lunch here in summer.

Doug is the chef with a menu that changes daily. I had ☛ veal, and I did not need a knife to cut it. Also had a cream of cauliflower soup that was excellent. Desserts, all homemade, are unusual and good. Rooms are large. The beds are very comfortable with ☛ feather pillows. How nice not to have a lump of foam under your head.

These two young people are trying very hard to succeed, and they are making it, especially with the help of two great inn dogs, Alex, a Siberian Husky, and Chuckey who is a Malemute.

How to get there: Take Exit 38 from I-93 to Route 117. The inn is about 3 miles up the hill on Route 117 just beyond The Homestead Inn.

⚖

E: Beds turned down at night always turn me on.

The cheers of millions are for politicians,
while the quiet appreciation of a well-cooked chop
is but for a few.

Olive Metcalf

Dexters
Sunapee, New Hampshire
03782

Innkeepers: Frank and Shirley Simpson
Telephone: 603-763-5571
Rooms: 17, all with private bath.
Rates: From May 1 to June 15, and all of September, $31 to
$43, per person, double occupancy, EPB. Rest of year,
$43 to $55, per person, double occupancy, MAP.
Facilities: Closed mid-October to December 26, and late
February to May 1. Breakfast, lunch in July and
August, dinner, bar. Tennis, swimming pool, recreation
barn. Fresh fruit and flowers in your room. No credit
cards accepted.

Your day starts with ☛ juice and coffee served in your
room at a time you set the night before. Or you can try being
really spoiled and have your complete breakfast served in
bed, but you will miss the lovely morning view of Lake
Sunapee from the dining room.

The lounge and bar are unique, with games, books, and
even a little shop just outside the door. The rooms at the inn

are a bit above average, with some carefully thought-out, unusual, wallpapers. The pillows are made of heavenly feathers, and plenty of them. Most of the beds are antiques that came down through the Simpson family.

The feature of the inn is tennis, and if you are a buff you will love it, for there are three fine courts. And after a game there is a large outdoor pool to cool off in.

For a good summer or fall activity there are some of the loveliest walking and hiking trails right on the inn property.

There is a special recreation room in the barn for all ages, but it is keyed to those under 16 who need a place of their own when the five o'clock cocktail hour begins.

How to get there: Take I-89 out of Concord and follow Exit 12 to Route 11, to 103B at Sunapee. Or take I-91 out of Spring-field and follow Exit 8 to Claremont, New Hampshire, to Route 103. The turn to the inn is marked by a sign 200 yards south of the intersection of 103 and 11. The inn is about 1½ miles off Route 103.

E: *Frank is a special innkeeper, right on top of everything.*

Tamworth Inn
Tamworth, New Hampshire
03886

Innkeepers: Larry and Kelly Hubbell
Telephone: 603-323-7721
Rooms: 21, ten with private bath.
Rates: Furnished upon request.
Facilities: Closed late March to mid-April, and late October to
   mid-November. Breakfast, dinner, Sunday brunch.
   Lunch served Tuesday through Saturday in summer,
   Saturdays only in winter. Bar, lounge, swimming pool.
   Trout fishing, skiing, and ice-skating nearby.

Tamworth is a large, rambling inn with a great deal of
charm, country charm. The common rooms are commodi-
ous and comfortable. There is a good library for books, tables
for games, and a nice bar and lounge for relaxing. The food
here is well above average.
   One cold winter night I can remember sitting in front of
a quiet fire, sipping a glass of wine, and trying to decide
which of the good food offerings I would have. I wound up
with ☛ Fettuccini Tamworth Inn. It is different from any

318

that I have ever had, and it is excellent. There are also two chicken dishes that are also different, one baked in honey and lemon, and the other topped with an Amaretto and tarragon cream sauce. They do creative things in this kitchen. At lunch one day the weather was cold, so the seafood puff usually served with a cold seafood salad was ☛ served hot, and, boy, was it good. Kelly does the cooking, and do try her Amaretto Grasshopper Pie. Delicious.

An interesting feature of the lower dining room walls is a frieze that looks like tin but is actually meticulously pressed cardboard.

Luncheon in the summertime is served in the patio by the pool.

The town of Tamworth is an old logging town. Masts for the king's ships were hauled down "Old Mast Road" by ox-cart. There are a lot of mountains here for you hikers and great streams for you trout fishermen.

How to get there: Route 25 in New Hampshire runs east and west above Lake Winnepesaukee. To the northeast of the lake, Route 113A runs off Route 25 to the north. The town of Tamworth is but two miles up the road.

E: I play the organ, and the Tamworth has a real oldie that still works just fine. I love it.

*If all inns were alike
they simply would not be inns.*

The Birchwood Inn
Temple, New Hampshire
03084

Innkeepers: Judy and Bill Wolfe
Telephone: 603-878-3285
Rooms: Seven, all share baths.
Rates: $30 to $35, single; $35 to $40, double; EPB.
Facilities: Closed one week in April. Dinner served Tuesday
  through Saturday. BYOB. Trout fishing, hiking, hunt-
  ing, golf, summer theater, and lakes nearby. No pets. No
  credit cards honored, but personal checks accepted.

The inn is in the Mount Monadnock region of New
Hampshire, so there is plenty to do and see here. From the
top of the mountain you can see four states, a nice reward for
you hikers. There are trout waiting for the fisherman, much
game for the hunter, plus all those good things for the quieter
type such as golf, summer theater, horseback riding and
walking.

Bill and Judy are the owner-chefs and are very good at
what they do. I understand from my spies that their
🖝 stuffed lobster is better than anywhere else. Chicken

Piccata and Shrimp Parmesan served on green noodles are two more examples of their good food. They have She-crab Soup which is hard to find north of South Carolina. It is excellent.

The inn has an 1878 square Steinway grand piano which is kept in perfect tune. The inn history stretches back some two centuries to circa 1775. During this time many people have come and gone, one notable personage being Henry David Thoreau. A room at the inn is named for Thoreau. Other rooms have rather different sort of names such as "The Bottle Shop" and "The School Room." The innkeepers will entertain you with the stories of how the rooms became so named.

How to get there: Take Route 2 west out of Boston to Fitchburg. Go north on Route 31 into New Hampshire to Greenville, and bear left on Route 45 to Temple.

E: *There is an inn cat named Sam. He rules the roost.*

The chill of a wood-stove-warmed bedroom
evaporates in the crisp smell of bacon for breakfast.

Kimball Hill Inn
Whitefield, New Hampshire
03598

Innkeepers: Penny and Rick Preston
Telephone: 603-837-2284
Rooms: Eight, three with private bath; one cottage.
Rates: $20 to $40, double occupancy, continental breakfast
   included.
Facilities: Closed November to May. Restaurant closed Tues-
   days. Lunch, dinner, bar, lounge. Gift shop. Swimming,
   riding, golf, and tennis nearby. American Express,
   MasterCard, and Visa accepted.

If you are looking for an inn that is comfortable, with
good food and ☛ a fantastic view, look no further. I sat in
the pub and had lunch looking out at the Presidential Range
to the east and the Green Mountains to the west. Beautiful!
The elevation of the inn is 1,390 feet.
   Preston's Pub is finished inside with old barn wood.
This is real barn-board, for they took down an old barn in
Lancaster, New Hampshire, washed the wood, and refurbished the interior of the inn with it. The result is warm and

cozy. If you look up you will see their 🖝 standard gauge American Flyer train make a loop around the pub on almost 100 feet of track. I love toy trains because I never grew up, and I am glad.

The dining room with its glorious views is pretty, serving good food. The pub also serves food. They have interesting Mountain Burgers, and a good chef's salad. The sweet and sour chicken is a different delight. There are also nice weekday specials in both the dining room and the pub.

For you inveterate shoppers they have a nice little gift shop right in the inn.

The rooms are comfortable, all different shapes and sizes, and all with spectacular views.

You will find many activities to entertain you a few miles down the road, or just sit in the pub and watch the world at peace.

How to get there: Take Route 116 east out of Littleton, New Hampshire toward Whitefield. The inn is one mile south of town on Kimball Hill Road.

E: 🖝 *The Mountain Rat is a special drink, and I mean special; orange, lemon, cranberry juice, light and dark rum, apricot brandy with 151-proof rum on top. It is served in a 22-ounce brandy snifter. Wow!*

Olive Metcalf

The Playhouse Inn
Whitefield, New Hampshire
03598

Innkeepers: Lucienne and Noel Lacan
Telephone: 603-837-2527
Rooms: 12, eight with private bath.
Rates: $22 to $42, double occupancy, EP. MAP rates
  available.
Facilities: Closed Mondays in spring and fall, and mid-
  October to mid-May. Breakfast, lunch in summer,
  dinner. Beer Garden, cocktail lounge, cabaret show in
  summer. Swimming pool. Golf and tennis nearby.
  MasterCard and Visa accepted.

With the Weathervane Theater just across the lawn,
Lucienne and Noel Lacan have taken the playhouse theme
for their delightful country inn. Noel is the chef, and the
menu, from Prelude through Curtain Calls, proves it in every
scene and act. There are those who hate vegetables, and then
there's me. Endives Meunière, Braised Heart of Celery, Lima
Bean Bretonne, Mushrooms Sauteed Provencale.
    The swimming pool, with its view of the mountains, is

lovely. There are six fireplaces in this comfortable old house. ☞ From the Backstage Bar to the Limelighter Restaurant, the theatrical touch is here, but with a really solid Gallic accent.

☞ Be sure to catch the enthralling cabaret held six nights a week in the Backstage Lounge. Five bouncingly talented youngsters—none are over 30—raise the rafters with song and merriment and bring a tear to more than one eye. Each evening offers an entirely different show, so feel free to go twice, or three times or more.

How to get there: Take I-93, then Route 3 into Whitefield. The inn is 1½ miles north of town on Route 3.

E: *The menu is great! Snails en Surprise have a new approach, and to finish off with Flaming Spanish coffee is indeed a switch.*

An unlit hearth in a good tavern is warmer by equators than a blazing fire where there is no love.

Olive Metcalf

Spalding Inn Club
Whitefield, New Hampshire
03598

Innkeepers: Ted and Topsy Spalding
Telephone: 603-837-2572
Rooms: 56, all with private bath and phone; 14 cottage suites.
Rates: Furnished upon request; AP.
Facilities: Closed mid-October to Memorial Day. Breakfast, lunch, dinner, bar, lounge. Swimming pool, four tennis courts, nine-hole par three golf course, 18-hole putting green, shuffleboard, lawn bowling. American Express, MasterCard, and Visa accepted.

I feel that everyone should at some time see how people lived years ago, and only in these special New Hampshire resorts can you live as our parents might have. I chose the smallest of these resorts that I could find, and it is just grand.

Set on 500 choice acres, this inn has remained in the same family for over fifty years. The service is ☛ impeccable. Tables are set with fingerbowls, silver napkin rings, and white linen. The food is excellent, and the choices are myriad. It reminds me of a cruise ship where you also have

326

unlimited food. Breakfast alone is outstanding; ☞ hot from the bakery popovers, doughnuts, and Danish pastries. I love how they say fresh *native* eggs. The luncheon menu is superb, and dinner, wow! Baked stuffed lobster, beef, veal, you name it and it is here. The desserts are totally sinful, and I wish I were back there right now.

The rooms are very comfortable with ☞ extra pillows and blankets. The cottages have living rooms, bedrooms, baths, and some even have their own porches. Fireplaces are in every cottage.

Downstairs is the TV lounge and bar. The TV screen is huge. This is a good spot to relax in. The main living room has a large stone fireplace, lots of books, and heaps of comfort. The inn also has a card room with a large collection of jigsaw puzzles. One puzzle or another is always being worked on by the guests.

There is so much to do here one need never leave the inn's 500 acres. The lawns are magnificent. You know ☞ Ted and Topsy are excellent innkeepers from the broad porch with grand rockers at hand. My mother told me about such places. It is wonderful that they are still here.

How to get there: Take I-93 north to Exit 41. Follow Route 116 through the village of Whitefield. Continue 1½ miles north of town, turn right onto Mountain View Road.

E: *Lawn bowling tournaments in both singles and doubles are held here. Have not seen this at any other inn.*

The Ram in the Thicket
Wilton, New Hampshire
03086

Innkeepers: Andrew and Priscilla Tempelman
Telephone: 603-654-6440
Rooms: Eight, three with private bath.
Rates: $20 to $25, single; $30 to $35, double; continental
   breakfast included.
Facilities: Open all year. Lunch served Wednesday to Friday
   in winter, Monday through Friday in summer. Dinner,
   bar. Indoor swimming pool, hiking. Summer theater
   nearby. MasterCard and Visa accepted.

The unusual name of the inn is taken from the old Bible
story of Abraham and Isaac. As a substitute for his son Isaac's
death, Abraham finds "a ram caught in the thicket" sent by
the Lord. Andrew and Priscilla founded the inn as a substitute for a life in the Midwest from which they wanted a
change.
   Luckily for all inn lovers the Tempelman's move has
resulted in another better-than-nice inn. This old Victorian
mansion has been carefully restored and now has lovely

dining rooms with crystal chandeliers, a hand-carved fireplace, and many other Victorian touches. One dining room has lovely blue delft tiles. The innkeepers are Dutch. The New Hampshire lounge has plants hanging from the ceilings.

Some of the luncheon dish names are great. They taste good, too. How about "Wandering Gypsy," a mélange of steamed vegetables napped with hearty Vermont cheddar cheese sauce, or "Year of the Ram Beef," marinated strips of beef, stir-fried with fresh vegetables. The dinner menu is just as inventive. There is a screened porch for summer dining.

This good inn is set in eight acres of wonderful country for roaming. You also have Frisky the cat and her three friends. Summer theater is close by. If you love to walk, there are many trails right at hand.

How to get there: Take Route 3 and just above Nashua take Exit 7 west on 101A to 101 about 15 miles to Wilton and watch for the inn signs.

E: ☛ *An enclosed swimming pool is my idea of heaven.*

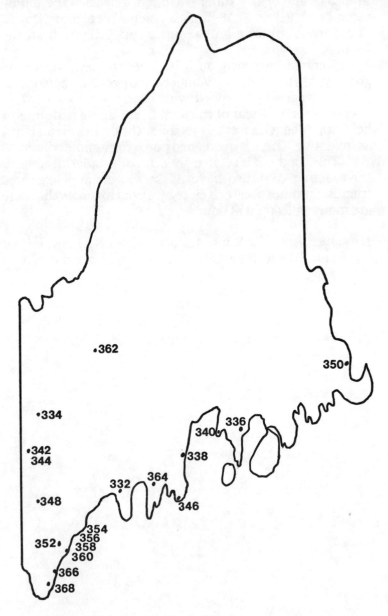

numbers on map refer to page numbers in this book

Maine

Olive Metcalf

Grane's Fairhaven Inn
Bath, Maine
04530

Innkeepers: Jane Wyllie and Gretchen Williams
Telephone: 207-443-4391
Rooms: Nine, one with private bath.
Rates: $20 to $30, single; $30 to $45, double; EP. Special
   packages for winter weekends.
Facilities: Open all year. Breakfast. BYOB lounge. Cross-
   country skiing, snowshoeing. No credit cards honored,
   but personal checks accepted.

"Truth is never pure and rarely simple. Better to wear
out than to rust out. Remember my friend, all things must
end." These are a few of the needlepoint sayings on the
☛ 14 steps going up the back stairs of this lovely old inn.
The ingenious rug was done by a former owner and the top
step is "Knowledge Grows by Steps." Only in a country inn
will you find things like this.

Rooms at Grane's are neat and very clean, with antiques, good beds, and wonderful views. The front of the inn
looks out on a salt tidal cove of the Kennebec River.

Breakfast is a thing of joy, with fresh fruit and souffles. I can still taste the hot bran muffins, and to top them off, the girls make their own jams and jellies. All this good eating is served in two lovely dining rooms.

The Tavern Library is a BYOB bar with fireplace, good chairs, and lots of fun. The English Bishop is a dandy hot drink for cold skiers. It is composed of port wine, oranges, cloves, honey, and brandy. If you have a cold it is just what the doctor, or a kindly bartender, ordered.

How to get there: The inn is 3½ miles from Route 1. From Route 1, just short of Bath, take the exit marked New Meadows. Turn right, go 7/10 mile; the road veers to the right sharply. Stay with the road; the golf course will be on your left, and the next road on the left is North Bath Road (8/10 mile from golf course). Take a left here, and the inn will be on your left in about a half mile.

E: *I have two cats, one Himalayan and one Maine Coon. At the inn is one Maine Coon, Cleo, and one bluepoint called Tuptim, and one flamepoint Himalayan called Foxie.*

> *When life dwindles thin and you wonder*
> *if the sun will rise on another day,*
> *seek perhaps an unfamiliar but rejuvenating bed*
> *in a nearby country inn.*

The Bethel Inn
Bethel, Maine
04217

Innkeeper: Dick Rasor; Manager Ray Moran
Telephone: 207-824-2175
Rooms: 65, all with private bath, phone; 16 with fireplace.
Rates: $39 to $62, per person, double occupancy, MAP.
Facilities: Open all year. Breakfast, lunch, dinner, bar, lounge. Golf, tennis, swimming pool, lake house with sailfish and canoes, cross-country skiing, sauna, indoor games, supervised activities for children. Own walking tour guide. Downhill skiing nearby. All major credit cards accepted.

The Bethel Inn faces the village common of Bethel, Maine, which is a National Historic District complete with beautifully restored churches, public buildings, and private homes. The rear of the inn overlooks its own 85 acres which include ☞ a nine-hole par 36 golf course.

Guest rooms have private baths and direct dial telephones. The rooms are well done and very comfortable.

The huge living room, music room, library are beautifully furnished for the utter comfort of the guests. The piano, by the way, is a Steinway.

Dining is a pleasure, either in the charming main dining room or on ☞ the fully screened porch overlooking the golf course. In winter dinner is served in the library which has a generous fireplace for your comfort.

Downstairs is the Mill Brook Tavern. Mill Brook cuts through the golf course and was the site of ☞ Twitchell's mill erected in the early 1700s in Sudbury, Canada, which is now Bethel, Maine.

Down here in the bar and lounge there is a light supper menu which is nice for the late hiker or skier. In the winter you can have hot cider, hot buttered rum, and glogg.

The lake house, three miles away on Lake Songo, features clambakes and barbeques. The downstairs patio on summer weekends also has a bar.

Skiing is super up here with Sunday River (I love that name) and Mount Abram right at hand. The inn has special ski packages. Do check them. And as ☞ a special special, they have over 20 kilometers of groomed cross-country trails for your pleasure.

How to get there: Bethel is located at the intersection of U.S. Route 2 and Maine Routes 5, 26, and 35. From the south take Exit 11 off the Maine Turnpike at Gray and follow Route 26 to Bethel. The inn is on the green.

E: Friday afternoon teas and Monday punch parties are nice.

olive Metcalf

Blue Hill Inn
Blue Hill, Maine
04614

Innkeepers: Jean and Fred Wakelin
Telephone: 207-374-2844
Rooms: Nine, all with private bath.
Rates: $38, double occupancy, EP.
Facilities: Open all year. Breakfast, dinner. BYOB. Swimming, tennis, golf, music, and cross-country skiing nearby. MasterCard and Visa accepted.

Harry is a big beautiful black Lab who greets all the people at the inn. This sort of tells you what to expect at this friendly place built in 1840. The rooms are impressive, with queen and king-sized beds so a tired body has enough room to really relax. The living and sitting rooms are furnished for extreme comfort, and there is a nook for BYOB cocktails. Guests also gather in the wicker corner of the dining room for a drink before dinner. You really will love every corner of this good inn.

This is a lovely section of Maine. Come any time of year, one season prettier than the next, and always things to do, 🐎 croquet on the lawn, and the famous potters, Rowantrees and Rackliff nearby. Or if you're a music lover, the nationally known Kneisel School of Music is at hand all summer. For winter there are 45 miles of cross-country trails in nearby Arcadia National Park on Mount Desert Island. The Blue Hill Country Club extends tennis, golf, and beach privileges to the guests of the inn.

Oh my, can they cook at this inn. One night I had 🐎 prime ribs, and they were done to perfection. 🐎 Popovers with the beef were delicious. Another guest said, "Too bad you were not here last night to taste the lemon meringue pie." He said it was the best he'd ever had, and I believe him. They were serving lamb the day I left. Believe me, I was sorry I had to move on.

How to get there: From Route 1 a bit east of Bucksport, take Route 15 right into Blue Hill.

E: 🐎 *This whole peninsula is perhaps the prettiest in Maine. You will love it.*

In the autumn, especially as one ages,
a firelit tavern in an excellent inn cannot be bettered
by the smallest mansions in Christendom.

Olive Metcalf

Camden Harbor Inn
Camden, Maine
04843

Innkeepers: Jim and Laureen Gilbert
Telephone: 207-236-4200
Rooms: 17, 12 with private bath.
Rates: $52 to $60, double occupancy, EPB.
Facilities: Open all year. Breakfast, dinner, Sunday brunch, bar. TV in lounge. Golf, skiing, sailing, and music nearby. MasterCard and Visa accepted.

Camden Harbor is one of the best-known ports in Maine, and one of the prettiest. Boats of yesteryear, both sail and power, as well as beautiful yachts of today, moor here by the rolling mountains that come right down to rocky shores. The inn sits up high above all of this and affords you a ☛ panoramic view all year round.

The rooms are rather small, but neat as a pin. The dining room has a fireplace and a very warm atmosphere. With the dining room is the ☛ Thirsty Whale Tavern, and no better spot for a touch or two, especially with the sounds of weekend folk music.

338

Several years ago, Jim enclosed the porch overlooking Penobscot Bay and the mountains with ceiling-high casement windows, to make a second dining room with a spectacular view.

There are walking tours, bicycle trips, and nature walks in and around Camden. There is hardly a spot in this whole lovely Maine town that is not worth a visit. In July the Penobscot Folk Festival draws crowds to the Rockport Opera House.

This is a wonderful town to muddle about in for days.

How to get there: From Route 1, which runs through the center of town, turn up Bayview Street to #83.

E: *Andre, the famous seal, lives in Rockport Harbor all summer. He winters at the aquarium in Boston and for 20 years has been swimming back on his own. Go see him. You will love him.*

Come back in 100 years and stay at my inn.

The Pentagöet Inn
Castine, Maine
04421

Innkeeper: Natalie F. Saunders
Telephone: 207-326-8616
Rooms: 12, five with private bath, two with half-bath.
Rates: $30 to $45, double occupancy, EP.
Facilities: Closed January through March. Breakfast, dinner, bar. Extensive wine list. Fishing, sailing, and golf nearby. American Express, MasterCard, and Visa accepted.

The Pentagöet is a lovely inn located on the unspoiled coast of beautiful Penobscot Bay. Built in 1894, this Victorian inn offers the traveler warmth and a very friendly atmosphere.

The living room holds many of Natalie's plants, has a wood-burning stove and comfortable places to just relax. The dining room serves breakfast and dinner. The chef prepares one entree each evening. ☛ Dinner is served in five courses. Seating is limited in order for you to enjoy the very best in dining.

The bedrooms are restful; some of them have little

alcoves with windows that allow you a view of the town and harbor. All in all a very nice part of the world to be in.

There is good Maine fishing, sailing, power boating, a nine-hole golf course, and dozens of islands nearby for delightful picnicking or just exploring. The Maine 🐾 Maritime Academy is here in Castine, and their training ship, State of Maine, is open to the public.

Bear, a Maine coon cat, and Spot, a black and white general breed, help run the inn. They really are in charge.

How to get there: Take Route 95 from Portland to the "Coastal Region—Brunswick, Bath, Route 1" Exit. Follow Route 1 to Bucksport and 2 miles beyond turn right onto Route 175. Take Route 175 to Route 166, which takes you into Castine.

⚓

E: The 🐾 *porch that overlooks the town and harbor and serves lunch and tea, and sometimes dinner, is my spot in summer.*

Trifles make an inn, but an inn is no trifle.

Center Lovell Inn
Center Lovell, Maine
04016

Innkeepers: Bil and Sue Mosca
Telephone: 207-925-1575
Rooms: Five, three with private bath.
Rates: $70.50 to $105, double occupancy, MAP.
Facilities: Closed March 15 to May 15, and October 15 to
    December 15. Box lunches available, dinner, service
    bar. Swimming and cross-country skiing. Downhill ski-
    ing nearby. MasterCard and Visa accepted.

Overlooking Kezar Lake in Center Lovell is a fine, gourmet country inn. People come from all over to sample Bil's
food, and no wonder. He features northern Italian cuisine at
its best. Veal Marsala, Veal Margarita, and Veal Parmigiano
Alforno are excellent and unusual. ☞ Pollo ala Nicolo Fir-
enze is boneless chicken with a different stuffing, baked and
basted with honey butter. And do try the shrimp or Maine
lobster. The pasta dishes are spectacular, but the house specialty is ☞ Lobster Fra Diavola di Center Lovell Inn. Two
days' reservation notice for this gem is worth it. Topping it all

off is fresh, rich, Italian cheesecake.

The recipes used here have been passed down through five traceable generations of Moscas and require the finest ingredients that money and knowledge can obtain. This is why Bil drives to Boston's North End every week. All of this fine food is served in a small, homey, and unpretentious dining room in front of a huge fireplace.

The front parlor has an almost original Hammond electric organ still in fine tune and a challenge to play. Here, too, is an 1870 firebox that my publisher fell in love with.

The porch goes around three sides of the inn. It overlooks the lake and in the summer you can dine out here. There are five downhill ski areas within half an hour, and you can cross-country from the back door. A beauty of a Labrador guards the inn. His name is Sabbetino. The area also offers fishing, canoeing, hiking, and the annual Fryeburg Fair in October.

How to get there: Coming either way on Route 302, turn north at Fryeburg, Maine onto Route 5. Fourteen miles north, the White Mountain Range will appear on your left, and the inn on your right.

E: ☛ *Three times a year, New Year's, Memorial Day and Columbus Day, the Moscas set aside three days for gourmandizing. From Friday through Sunday you eat and forget diet.*

*A day be the fire, a hot ale in hand,
and the idiot cares of the world are as nothing.*

Westways Country Inn
Center Lovell, Maine
04016
(For reservations: P.O. Box 357, Sudbury, MA 01776)

Innkeepers: Don and Barbara Tripp
Telephone: 207-926-2663, 800-225-4897, 617-235-3327
  (Mass. call collect)
Rooms: Seven, one with private bath, two with half-bath;
  two cottages.
Rates: $90 to $116, double occupancy, MAP. Package plans
  available.
Facilities: Closed Thanksgiving and Christmas, April and
  May. Breakfast, dinner, full license. Swimming, boat-
  ing, sailing, tennis, handball, recreation building with
  bowling, Ping-Pong, pool, and card room. Two marinas
  on Lake Kezar. MasterCard and Visa accepted.

Westways was built in the 1920s as the executive retreat of the Diamond Match Company. It is a look into the
past that is a pure delight.
  The living room overlooking Kezar Lake is large. There
is a huge stone fireplace and comfortable couches and chairs.

On cool nights in winter your ☛ five-course dinner is served in here on glorious ☛ Spode china. The appetizers might be quiche or stuffed mushrooms. The soup may be stracciatella. Your salad is served with homemade dressings, and the entrees consist of two nightly choices. The day I was there one of the choices was lobster. But your choice may be Veal Cordon Bleu, or fresh red snapper, prime ribs, or steak. Great, creative desserts and coffees come next. This is indeed the way to live.

All of the rooms are gracious, most overlook the lake, and all have ☛ libraries. The president of Diamond Match was a prolific reader, and his collection is here for you to enjoy. By the way, all of the rooms are different, some have wicker headboards and some have four-poster beds. All are comfortable.

The boathouse overlooks the lake and is comfortable for reading or just idle meditation. ☛ The view of the White Mountains from here is fantastic. There are over 100 acres in all that go with the inn, plus a sandy beach, and a picnic area where a sea plane once was kept. The inn dog is, are you ready for this, Ding-a-ling. Absolutely loved her.

How to get there: Coming either way on Route 302 turn north at Fryeburg, Maine onto Route 5. Fourteen miles north the lake will appear on your left, and the inn entrance (marked with a sign) is on your left about 6 miles up the lake.

E: *There is* ☛ *a body shower in the bath on the first floor that is unbelievable. It is certainly one-of-a-kind.*

The Craignair Inn
Clark Island, Maine
04859

Innkeepers: Norman and Terry Smith
Telephone: 207-594-7644
Rooms: 17, all with private bath.
Rates: $30 to $35, per person, double occupancy, MAP.
Facilities: Open all year. Breakfast, dinner for six or more in
   winter. Special diets furnished upon reasonable notice.
   BYOB. Swimming, skiing, tennis, riding, and golf near-
   by. MasterCard and Visa accepted.

This isn't a fancy inn, but it is comfortable. It was built
about 50 years ago as a boarding house for quarry workers. It
is hung on the edge of the water, with rocks, tidal flats, an
ocean inlet, and loads of peace and quiet. The quarry has
long since been worked out, but you can swim there in the
salt water that rises and falls with the tide. If you worry about
old wooden buildings, sleep relaxed here.

There is always something to do at Craignair. If the fog
rolls in, cozy up to the fire in the sitting room. When it snows,
the Camden Snow Bowl Ski Area is a short drive away.

Nearby towns and villages offer diversified activity stops, including antiques shops, art galleries, museums, and specialty shops. Or you could attend a concert, golf, play tennis, ride horseback, bicycle, sail, or catch one of the numerous ☞ festivals paying homage to seafood, blueberries, chicken, sailboats, and history.

If tidal pools, clam flats, islands, meadows, and spruce forests invite you, come to Craignair in any season.

No excuse now, if you are a weight watcher, or on a salt-free diet. ☞ Terry will stick to your diet if you let her know a day or two ahead of time. There's one entree only each evening, but what variety. And on Saturday, enjoy that traditional Maine dinner, fresh lobster with steamers. The dining room is cozy, done in blue and white with lots of windows looking to the sea.

How to get there: Go to Thomaston on Route 1, then take Route 131 south for about 6 miles, and turn left on Route 73 for about a mile to Clark Island Road. Take a right, and the inn is at the end of the road.

E: *The living room-library is very comfortable. This is a real Maine Coast inn with its own Maine Coast dog, a black Lab named Delia.*

Having had an excellent meal and a lovely evening,
I tucked myself in bed knowing I had sinned
but it did not seem to matter.

The Carriage Inn
Cornish, Maine
04020

Innkeepers: Colonel T. J. and Suzy Owens
Telephone: 207-625-4042
Rooms: Four, three with private bath.
Rates: $30 to $48, double occupancy, continental breakfast
   included.
Facilities: Open all year. Full breakfast, lunch, dinner. Full
   liquor license, dress and gift shop. Canoeing and fishing
   nearby. All major credit cards accepted.

The inn was built in 1840 and was the original Cornish
Inn. Over the years it fell into disrepair and was, just before
T. J. and Suzy bought it, a poor rooming house. These two
have done a wonderful restoration job. I saw the inn before
and could hardly believe the after.

Beautiful, undamaged ◢ tin ceilings are in every
room on the first floor and even run up under the stairs. The
two dining rooms have bay windows, bow Windsor chairs,
and white napery. China and silverware are by Dansk, and
all glasses are stemware. This is the right way to set a table.

Suzy is the chef and she serves country French food that is delicious. One of her dishes is ☛ Boeuf-à-la-mode, and it is excellent. She also makes a wicked chocolate mousse.

Some of the rooms have wood-burning fireplaces, and all have designer sheets and ☛ big thirsty towels. There are a queen-sized and a twin bed in each room.

Up on the third floor is a sundeck with a marvelous view of the White Mountains and way off in the distance, Mount Washington. Suzy is also ☛ a dress designer, and her beautiful things are for sale here at the inn.

T. J. is in charge of the pub. He is a properly, though not completely, reformed Irishman who makes a great barkeep.

There is canoeing on the Saco and Ossipie rivers which are close by.

The inn cat, Fuzz-E, has his own secret door in one of the dining rooms. You must look for it, but do watch out, for from time to time Fuzz-E arrives with a cat friend.

How to get there: From Portland, Maine take Route 25 west for about 35 minutes. The Carriage Inn is right in Cornish, next to the library, on your right.

🐟🐟

E: *Suzy and T. J. have put so much of themselves into the inn that it warms my heart.*

olive Metcalf

Lincoln House Country Inn
Dennysville, Maine
04628

Innkeepers: Mary Carol and Gerald Haggerty
Telephone: 207-726-3953
Rooms: Six, all share four semi-private baths; two with wood
   stove, two with fireplace.
Rates: $40 to $45, double occupancy, EP.
Facilities: Open all year. Closed Mondays for food. Breakfast
   for house guests, dinner by reservation. Dinner served
   only Fridays and Saturdays from November 1 to May
   31. Full bar, wine list, entertainment. No pets. Master-
   Card and Visa accepted.

When you walk in the side door of the inn you are in
what once was the summer kitchen and now is a library full
of books with a huge fireplace hung with old cooking equipment and one Japanese wok! On through Mary Carol's
kitchen you find two delightful dining rooms. Beyond is a
large living room with a baby grand piano. This is an inn
where you can feel totally at home.
   Mary Carol's kitchen really turns out exceptional food,

best ☞ lamb I ever had. It was prepared quite differently and only Mary Carol can tell you how. Her breakfast muffins almost outdo her lamb.

The inn is a handsome, yellow, foursquare Georgian Colonial perched above the Denny River, one of the few rivers where you can find the Atlantic salmon. John Audubon once stayed here and was so impressed he named the "Lincoln Sparrow" for his hosts. The inn was built by an ancestor of President Lincoln in 1787.

Jerry is a master restorer and perfectionist. It shows all over the inn. The woodshed, a village pub, has ☞ a bar that Jerry carved from a 4,000-pound elm trunk with a bear's head carved at one end. The woodshed has fun on Thursday nights in the winter. It is "open mike" time and all local amateurs come and do their thing. Sundays it is international dart shoots with neighboring Canada. The U.S. seems to always win and whether this is their ability or Jerry's liberal beers we do not know.

You will love this inn, but it is a long way off, so do make reservations ahead.

How to get there: Route 1 goes right by Dennysville. Driving up take the second sign into Dennysville, just after you have crossed the Dennys River. Turn left and you will find the inn almost immediately on your right.

🍐

E: ☞ *Bald eagles and osprey are seen here, and families of seals swim in the river. It is a long way up here but worth every mile.*

The Kennebunk Inn
Kennebunk, Maine
04043

Innkeepers: Arthur and Angela LeBlanc
Telephone: 207-985-3351
Rooms: 35, 12 with private bath, all with air conditioning.
Rates: Off season, $26 to $38; In season, $30 to $45; double
    occupancy; EP.
Facilities: Open all year. Closed Christmas Day. Full breakfast
    June to October 15; continental breakfast off season.
    Lunch and dinner (except on Sunday). Bar, lounge.
    Fishing and swimming nearby. All major credit cards
    accepted.

    The inn is located right smack on Route 1 in the heart of
town convenient to everything. Even the beaches are but a
bit away.
    Dating back to 1799, the inn was in total disrepair when
the LeBlancs bought it. With a tremendous amount of work
and attention to detail, they have restored the inn to its
current state of being a proper in-town country inn.
    All of the beds have ☞ new mattresses and all bed-

rooms are air-conditioned. A modern touch like air-conditioning in an old inn is great. There are some brass headboards, and if I know Angela, there will be more. Throughout the inn the wallpapers are French imports, and they are beautiful.

The upstairs foyer is a nice spot to gather. There are couches and chairs, TV, puzzles, games, and books.

The dining room has colorful tablecloths, and the food served here is impeccable. For breakfast, among many dishes, is Omar Pacha, baked eggs on sauteed onions and topped with cheese. Another dish is King Neptune's Delight, two fresh eggs enthroned on crab meat on English muffins and crowned with hollandaise sauce. There are also ☞ croissants and scones baked daily. Luncheon is equally interesting. One item is a one-half pound hamburger made of charbroiled choice beef. Delicious. For dinner do try Angela's Veal Under Glass or her husband's King Arthur's Sirloin Steak. You will love whatever you order.

How to get there: Take Exit 3 from I-95 (the Maine Turnpike) to Kennebunk. The inn is at 45 Main Street.

⛵

E: *The Saturday night feature is flambé duck with the chef's choice of a liqueur sauce. It is served at table-side with flaming brandy.*

How good of you to have asked me in.

Captain Lord Mansion
Kennebunkport, Maine
04046

Innkeepers: Beverly Davis and Rick Litchfield
Telephone: 207-967-3141
Rooms: 16, all with private bath, 11 with working fireplace.
Rates: $64 to $84, double occupancy, continental breakfast
   included.
Facilities: Open all year. Breakfast only meal served. BYOB.
   Perkins Cove and Rachel Carson Wildlife Refuge near-
   by. No children under 12. No credit cards honored, but
   personal checks accepted.

   I keep looking for a word to do justice to describing this
inn. Exquisite is not enough. One of the beds is a four-poster
12 feet high. Rugs and wallpaper, thanks to Beverly's eye,
are well coordinated, ☞ thirsty towels are abundant, and
extra blankets and pillows help make your stay better than
pleasant.
   Eleven of the guest rooms have working fireplaces.
There are 14 throughout the inn. Most of the rooms have

padded, deep window seats, a great place to relax and day-dream.

Throughout the inn are portraits of past owners in the Lord family. There is still some of the original Lord furniture. A handsome dining room table with carved feet and chairs belonged to Nathaniel Lord's grandson, Charles Clark, and is dated 1880. The wallpaper in one bedroom that is still beautifully intact dates also from 1880. The paper in the front bedroom goes back to 1812.

Breakfast is the only meal served, and it is a rare treat. You eat at a huge table in the center of a kitchen that has about as big a wood stove as we have seen. For other meals there are many fine restaurants in Kennebunkport.

This is a bring-your-own-bottle inn, and from the scenic cupola on its top to the parlors on the first floor, you will find many great places to enjoy a drink.

How to get there: From I-95 take Exit 3 to Kennebunk. Turn left on Route 35 and drive through Kennebunk to Kennebunkport. Turn left at the traffic light at the Sunoco station. Go over drawbridge and take first right onto Ocean Avenue. Go 3/10 mile and turn left at the Mansion. Park behind the building and take brick walkway to guest entrance.

⧗

E: *Rick knows the history of the house and loves to tell it as it was, so do ask him.*

Ol've Metcalf

English Meadows Inn
Kennebunkport, Maine
04046

Innkeepers: Gene, Helene, and Claudia Kelly
Telephone: 207-967-5766
Rooms: 14, two with private bath.
Rates: $30, single; $45 to $55, double; EPB.
Facilities: Closed November 1 to April 1. Full breakfast only
    meal served. BYOB. Antique shop. One mile from
    ocean. No credit cards honored, but personal checks
    accepted.

This is another breakfast-only inn, a type that we are
just beginning to include. Here in Kennebunkport there are
plenty of restaurants for you to choose from, so you'll have
no problem finding a good place to eat.

English Meadows is a lovely Victorian farmhouse, circa
1840. The inn has antiques, brass and iron beds, and hooked
rugs. The carriage house is paneled and has a large fireplace
in the gracious living room. There is much wicker furniture
that has bright gray covers on the cushions. This is a nice
place to relax after a day of fun.

At English Meadows you are only five minutes from Dock Square where you will find good restaurants, public golf courses, churches, galleries, and deep sea fishing. ☛ A bicycle is a great piece of equipment to bring along to Kennebunkport. While the area has some gently rolling hills, you will not find backbreaking slopes to negotiate. The beach for you to use is only a mile from the inn.

At the inn is "The Whalers Antique Shop" where you will find country furniture and accessories, beautiful quilts, hooked rugs, baskets, and much interesting wicker work.

The inn is situated on six acres of meadow and pine land and has been operating as an inn for over eighty years.

How to get there: From the Maine Turnpike take Exit 3 to Kennebunk. Follow Route 35 south, toward the ocean. The inn is 5 miles along on the right.

☾

E: *My heart got taken by one of the inn cats, Kee, some kind of Maltese.*

A well-run inn and a man on a diet
go together about as well as
an arsonist and a bale of hay.

Old Fort Inn
Kennebunkport, Maine
04046

Innkeepers: David and Sheila Aldrich
Telephone: 207-967-5353
Rooms: 12, all with private bath, kitchen, and TV. One suite.
Rates: $50 to $80, double occupancy, continental breakfast
    included.
Facilities: Closed end of October to May 1. Suite available all
    year. Continental breakfast only meal served. BYOB.
    Swimming pool, tennis, antique shop. Bikes for rent,
    ocean nearby. All major credit cards accepted.

When you enter the Old Fort Inn you are in an excellent antique shop. Next you are in a huge living room that
overlooks the swimming pool. The pool has ☞ a solar cover
that enables the inn to stretch its swimming season a bit. I
know it works because I have one on my pool. This is a
lovely, comfortable living room with a fireplace, a super spot
to curl up and read a book.

The rooms are charming, and all are fully equipped
with a kitchen. This is so nice when you plan a longer stay

than overnight. The beds have antique headboards of brass or wood along with good, comfortable mattresses. The towels are ☞ color-coordinated, which I always love. There is a nice library in the foyer.

The inn does provide ☞ a laundry. Until you have been on the road a week or so, you do not know how convenient such a facility is. The inn also provides a place to shower and change if you are checking out and still want to swim in the pool or the ocean that is only one block away.

There is a TV in each room, and the suite has color cable. To go with these modern touches is the inn cat, Samantha. And to go with the cat is the great inn child, Shana. She is some innkeeper. You will love her.

Although you may want to prepare your own food in your fully equipped kitchen, the inn does provide you with the menus of all the area restaurants.

How to get there: Take Exit 3 from the Maine Turnpike (it is marked Kennebunk), turn left on Route 35 to Kennebunkport, and follow the signs to the inn. It is on Old Fort Avenue.

♦♦♦

E: *The spiral staircase at one end of the inn is neat.*

Village Cove Inn
Kennebunkport, Maine
04046

Innkeepers: Jacques and Carol Gagnon
Telephone: 207-967-3993
Rooms: Four, one with private bath; 30 in annex, all with private bath; all the rooms have air conditioning and TV. One cottage.
Rates: $46 to $55, per person, double occupancy, MAP.
Facilities: Open all year. Breakfast, dinner, bar, Sunday brunch in spring, fall, and winter. Pools inside and out, exercise room. All major credit cards accepted.

The Village Cove Inn is a contemporary inn nestled in the trees on a hillside overlooking Chick's Cove, just a few minutes from Dock Square. Fun to watch the tide in Chick's Cove. It is an honest Maine tide that really runs.

From the outside pool there's quite a view. What a delighful place to just relax and enjoy. ☞ The inside pool is solar heated; how nice to swim in 80° water while you watch the snow fall outside. In winter the large function room by the pool becomes an exercise room, a unique feature for a country inn.

The inn staff conducts art workshops all year, watercolors, oils, pencil, and pastels, and, except for the summer, gourmet cooking classes are also held.

The old canoe landing is the restaurant with a wonderful array of food. There are five appetizers, and do try the Mussels Marinara. They are steamed in white wine with a hint of garlic, fresh parsley, and shallots. The inn's Coquille St. Jacques Mornay is different and delicious, baked scallops, shrimp, and fresh mushrooms in a delicate wine and cheese sauce. The bouillabaisse is really chock-full of good things from the sea. Lobster, of course, is king here and is served however you may wish it. I was lucky enough to be here for a wine-tasting party, and I know the wines are good. I do believe I tried most of them.

The Ledge Room and the lounge are unique in that they seem to nestle themselves right into the rockbound coast of Maine. The spiral staircase goes from the restaurant around down to the bar. It is a good trip.

How to get there: From Kennebunk follow Route 9 or 9-A into Kennebunkport where the two roads join. Continue on Route 9 until it turns right at Main Street. Stay on Main Street after Route 9 leaves you on the left. Bear right at the fork, and the inn is three-quarters of a mile along on your right. Just follow the inn's yellow signs.

E: *The inn is more modern than you might expect, but I could not leave it out of the book. Try it, and you will see why.*

Winter's Inn
Kingfield, Maine
04947

Innkeeper: Michael Thom
Telephone: 207-265-5421
Rooms: 12, nine with private bath.
Rates: $50 to $60, per person, MAP. 21-day cancellation
notice. EP rates and whitewater rafting packages
available.
Facilities: Inn open all year. Dining room closed in May and
June, and first three weeks of November. Breakfast,
dinner, Sunday brunch in summer, bar, lounge. Swimming pool, tennis, cross-country skiing. Downhill skiing, hunting, fishing, hiking, golf, whitewater rafting,
and canoeing nearby. MasterCard and Visa accepted.

Located in the heart of the western Maine mountains,
Bigelow, Sugarloaf, and Saddleback, sits Winter's Inn on top
of a ten-acre hill on the edge of town. It is a restored neo-
Georgian manor house, built at the turn of the century for
Amos Greene Winter. The house had fallen into sad disrepair
when it was rescued in 1972 by Michael Thom, a young

architect from Cambridge, Massachusetts, and Toronto, Canada. ☞ Much to his pride, the building has now been listed on the National Register of Historic Places.

Elegant without being stiff or pretentious, the inn has been decorated with ☞ handsome wallpapers. The walls are hung with a fine collection of oil paintings and gold-framed mirrors. The view from the dining room windows of the western mountains is breathtaking. The view is the same from the swimming pool.

☞ Food served in Le Papillon is delightful, a continuing surprise in this faraway inn at the back of beyond. Guests can spend their days climbing mountains, come home to the inn for a swim and a drink, then dress for dinner and dine elegantly, savoring the best of both worlds.

Hunting, fishing, hiking along the Appalachian Trail, and canoeing welcome outdoors people. Downhill skiers are especially happy here, but so is the lady guest ensconced by the pool with her needlepoint or book.

Balthazar's Pub is an elegant place to have a drink, play backgammon, chat, and enjoy. There is a unique corner fireplace in here.

How to get there: Kingfield is halfway between Boston and Quebec City, and the Great Lakes area and the Maritimes. Take the Maine Turnpike to the Belgrade Lakes Exit in Augusta. Follow Highway 27 through Farmington to Kingfield. The inn is on a small hill near the center of town.

E: *There lives here an inn cat, Balthazar. He is orange and white and as regal as his name. Once I had a look-alike cat, Alleycat, just as majestic.*

The Newcastle Inn
Newcastle, Maine
04553

Innkeepers: George and Sandra Thomas
Telephone: 207-563-5685
Rooms: 20, nine with private bath.
Rates: $29 to $35, double occupancy, EP.
Facilities: Open all year. Breakfast. TV in sitting room, antique shop. Swimming and cross-country skiing nearby. No credit cards accepted.

Found on each bed here at the inn is this greeting, ☞ "We bid you warm welcome as you enter this room. It may not be our good fortune to come to know you this trip, but we want you to feel this is your home while away, and that we are eager for your comfort and happiness while our guest. May you rest well. May you be healthy under this roof. May your stay fulfill your every expectation. May God bless and prosper you."

The lovely porch full of ☞ wicker furniture is always cool in summer and is a nice way to enter this charming inn. Breakfast is the only meal being served now, but what a breakfast, best French toast I have ever found. The dining room is charming. There is a large, comfortable living room with fireplace and another room for TV viewing.

Rooms here are Maine-size small, but are well done with white bedspreads, white curtains, and they are clean, clean, clean.

At the inn you are within walking distance of the lovely town of Damariscotta and its salt-water tidal river. You are also within short driving distance of the famous Pemaquid peninsula with its lighthouse, fort, and beach. In the other direction you are not far from Boothbay Harbor. Do come up and enjoy this distinctive part of Maine.

How to get there: When going north on Route 1, take the Newcastle exit to the right. Stay to your left; the inn is about 4 blocks down the road on River Road.

⚓

E: Good cross-country skiing is all around you, so do come up.

*The glowing carriage lamp beside the door
of a country inn when viewed through a cold rain
erases the rigors of the day
and promises a fine, fine evening.*

olive Metcalf

The Old Village Inn
Ogonquit, Maine
03907

Innkeepers: Frederick L. Thomas and Alf B. Kristiansen
Telephone: 207-646-7088
Rooms: Six suites, one double, all with private bath.
Rates: In summer, $35, double room, $55, suites; rest of year,
$22.50, double, $30, suites; double occupancy, EP.
Facilities: Closed January and February. Dining room closed
Mondays in winter. Breakfast in summer, lunch, din-
ner, bar. TV, game room. Fishing, swimming, and the-
ater nearby. MasterCard and Visa accepted.

Fred Thomas and Alf Kristiansen have a good in-town
inn that has a history going back to 1833. Interestingly, part
of its history was the August 2, 1942 issue of the ☞ *Saturday
Evening Post*, which had for its cover a picture of the inn done
by John Falter.

The inn is always being updated, and now there are six
suites available. One of the bedrooms has a headboard made
from four ladder-back chairs. According to Fred it is the only
one of its kind. He should know, because he built it.

The bar is a real, English country pub with hanging stemware glasses, small tables, and a cooking unit off to one side. The dining rooms are different and comfortable. One is enclosed in a greenhouse, with a view of the ocean and with greenery everywhere. The Bird & Bottle is another dining room, and the newest is the enclosed porch that wraps around the front of the inn.

The Ogunquit Room is a perfect spot for a private party of up to 20 people. There is a living room with a TV, nice for the younger set, and also a room with piano and game tables.

Hard on the rock-bound coast of Maine, this inn has interests for all. The famous Ogunquit Playhouse is here, as is the newer off-Broadway repertory theater. There is plenty of fishing and swimming, and two unusual walking trails.

The Marginal Way winds you along the spectacular bay and sea, and the Trolley Trail follows an abandoned line through the woods. I have never gone by, or even near, Ogunquit without a stop at this good inn.

How to get there: The inn is at 30 Main Street in the middle of Ogunquit. Main Street is Route 1.

E: *The greenhouse is so nice. I have one at home, so I know.*

York Harbor Inn
York Harbor, Maine
03911

Innkeepers: Joe and Garry Dominguez
Telephone: 207-363-5119
Rooms: Ten, all share baths.
Rates: $35 to $55, double occupancy, continental breakfast
   included.
Facilities: Open all year. Breakfast, dinner, Sunday brunch,
   bar, cocktail lounge. Entertainment on weekends. Public beach, fishing, boating, golf, tennis. American Express, MasterCard, and Visa accepted.

Wow! Three dining rooms all with a 🖝 view of the
Atlantic. This is a cozy and comfortable inn with good food
and good grog. A unique touch is the cellar lounge with 🖝 a
poetry corner for special readings. The lounge has a nice bar
and a small dance floor.
   The inn is old, 1637 being the date for the room into
which you first come. It was a fisherman's house and has
sturdy beams in the ceiling, not for holding up the roof, but

rather to hold up wet sails so they could dry before the large fireplace.

Everything is 🖝 made to order and baked here. Baked, stuffed mussels are but one of the great appetizers. There is always a soup of the day. Six different salads and the pasta offerings make my mouth water just writing about them. There is plenty of good Maine seafood, and, of course, beef, veal, and poultry. The chef also creates his own special of the day. Be sure to ask what it is if the waitress should fail to mention it. Delicious, homemade desserts top off the good meals, followed by a wide menu of special coffees.

The rooms are comfortable and almost all have a good view of the sea. On a quiet night you can hear the sea breaking on the generous beach below the inn. A wonderful way to have a relaxing night of good sleep.

How to get there: From I-95 take the Yorks Berwicks Exit. Turn right at the blinking light, left at the first traffic light (Route 1A), and go through the village about 3 miles. The inn is on the left.

♒

E: *York Harbor and all the areas around are beautiful. Be sure to bring your camera so you can remember it all at home.*

> *I was lost, I was tired, I was discouraged,*
> *and then I found a friendly inn.*

And Just a Bit South of New England

The coast of New England is girded by famous, old Route 1, and it seemed a pity to ignore this grand highway when it leaves Connecticut and plunges into New York. If you follow it for its entire length you will find a sign that says, "Route 1, Mile 0." It is against a fence in Key West, Florida. Immediately to your right at the end of Duval Street is The Pier House.

This is old Key West where a sunset is a celebrated daily habit. A man with an iguana strolls by or you listen to a congo beat, or you watch incredible magic shows. It is all here at Mallory Square every day. Or you can enjoy the sunset at The Pier House, sipping a cool drink in their ☛ rooftop bar. It is very comfortable up here watching the rituals of the world's greatest sunsets.

The guest rooms and suites are sumptuous. The ☛ terraces afford you unmatched views, and the food ranges from the elegant gourmet cuisine of The Pier House restaurant to the conch fritters served in a paper basket at the outdoor bar. Their ☛ Key Lime Pie, I know from experience, is a thing of joy. None better. And oh, those stone crabs!

I do believe you can tell I like it down here, not a country inn but a beautiful resort. Write or call for rates 1-800-327-8340. The Pier House is at One Duval Street. Air Florida jets you there from Miami in 35 minutes. I have driven down about 25 times. It is an interesting trip. Take your choice of car or plane, but do go.

Index

Other Globe Pequot Books
for your further travelling pleasure

Guidebooks:
A Guide to New England's Landscape
Factory Store Guide to All New England
Guide to Martha's Vineyard
Guide to Nantucket
Guide to New Bedford, Massachusetts
The Best of the Berkshires
Handbook for Beach Strollers
Historic Walks in Old Boston
Guide to the Ski Touring Centers of New England
In and Out of Boston with (or without) Children

Short Walk Books:
On Long Island
In Connecticut
On Cape Cod

Short Bike Ride Books:
In Connecticut
On Long Island
In Greater Boston and Central Massachusetts
On Cape Cod, Nantucket and the Vineyard
In the Berkshires
In Rhode Island

Available at your bookstore or direct from the publisher. For a free catalogue of New England books, write: The Globe Pequot Press, Old Chester Road, Chester, Connecticut 06412

About the author

The "inn creeper" is the nickname Elizabeth Squier has earned in her almost 11 years of researching this guide to the inns of New England. And a deserved name it is, for she tours more than 200 inns every year from top to bottom, inside out, before recommending the best ones to you.

A recognized authority on fine food and lodging, Elizabeth is a gourmet cook and has written travel and food columns for many periodicals. Like you, she recognizes readily the special ingredients that make a good inn exceptional.